BOUND TO FORGIVE

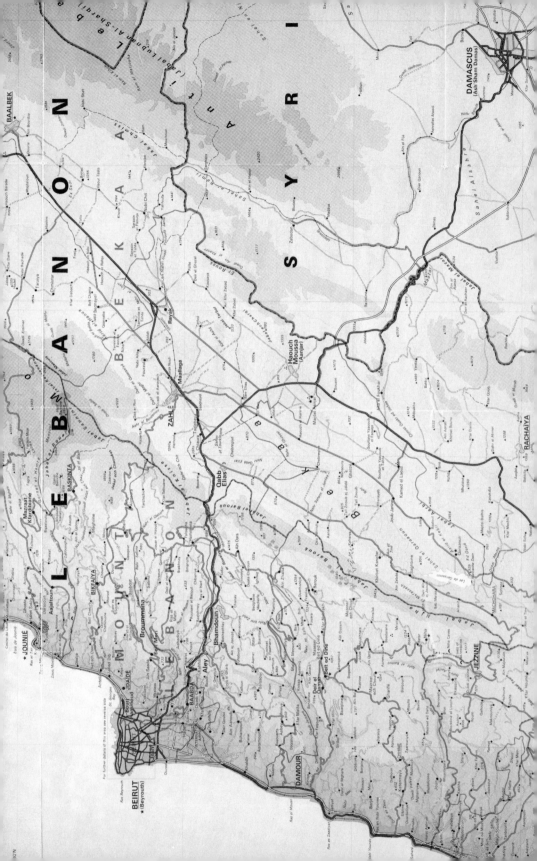

BOUND TO FORGIVE

FORGIVE

*The Pilgrimage to Reconciliation
of a Beirut Hostage*

Lawrence Martin
Jenco, O.S.M.

AVE MARIA PRESS   Notre Dame, Indiana 46556

© 1995 by Ave Maria Press, Inc.

International Standard Book Number: 0-87793-554-8

Library of Congress Catalog Card Number: 95-75315

Cover design and illustration by Elizabeth J. French

Printed and bound in the United States of America.

To my sisters and brothers
To relatives and friends
To all who worked to secure my release
and prayed me home

ACKNOWLEDGEMENTS

I am very grateful to Chris Codol and Frank Cunningham who so generously with their time and talents helped me put back the "adjectives."

CONTENTS

FOREWORD

For eight years, from 1984 to 1991, more than a dozen men shared in various combinations a series of tiny, often dark and filthy cells in Lebanon. A decade later, most of the survivors have written books about that experience (including myself).

Nearly the same things happened to each of us, often at the same time and in the same place. Yet each of those accounts is very different. Not just different in the sense that our perceptions of what was happening to and around us were not the same, or because we remember facts or occasions differently. The accounts are different in their essence. "Each of us had to reach inside himself to find that which was necessary to survive," Brian Keenan told me in a conversation after we were all home and free.

The accounts, therefore, are more about ourselves than about the experiences we shared. As we were different men, so are they different.

This book is a true account of my friend and brother, Lawrence Martin Jenco. He is not a saint, not quite. The occasional sharp edge of his very human tongue, which as the only Catholic member of the Church of the Locked Door, I felt from time to time, is here. So are the doubts and fears we shared for so long.

But mainly his account is filled with gentleness, as he is. The love for others that spills from him flows also from these pages. Most of all, his faith in a kind and loving God shines brilliantly, as it does always in his presence.

Father Jenco has taught me many things about myself, about forgiveness and humility, about how love for God demands that we love our brothers, even those who believe themselves our enemy.

In this book, he continues the lesson.

TERRY ANDERSON

9

INTRODUCTION

During the days of my captivity I thought of writing a book about those times. I did not want to undertake it alone, however. I wanted it to be a collaborative effort with Servite brother, mentor, and friend Neal Flanagan. Neal was a scripture scholar who taught at the Franciscan School of Theology of the Graduate Theological Union in Berkeley, California.

But I would find out strangely and unexpectedly that Neal had died while I was a hostage. As we flew home to the U.S. from Europe after my release, I asked my sister Mae about Neal. She turned to me and said "Neal died." I assumed she was talking about another Neil in my life, Neil Callahan, who had died just before I was taken hostage. I thought Mae simply did not understand I was aware of Neil Callahan's death. Distracted by something else, I made no further inquiry.

Later at home in Joliet, while mulling over a newspaper article, it occurred to me I had not yet heard from my other Neal. I wondered out loud to Mae, "Why do you think Neal Flanagan never called?"

"I told you," she said, "he died. He had a heart attack while driving home from a heart therapy session in Berkeley and drove into a tree."

At that instant any desire I ever had to write a book died as well.

Several years later I was scheduled to give a speech at Trinity College in Burlington, Vermont. While sitting in the college library working on my talk, I looked up at a stack of books facing me. One in particular caught my eye—*The Plague* by Albert Camus. One of several books the guards had given us in captivity, seeing it again quickened my desire to write of my experiences.

11

I remembered that a character in Camus' novel, one Joseph Grand, had struggled to write, unable to find the words. He strained with the opening sentence, refining and rewriting endlessly. Grand confided to the novel's main character, Dr. Bernard Rieux, that once he succeeded "in rendering perfectly the picture in my mind's eye," he knew he would be satisfied and could say "hats off!"

In time, Grand was struck by the plague ravaging the city and lay dying. Rieux inquired about his writing. Grand asked to be given the manuscript from the drawer where he kept it. Receiving it, he pressed its fifty pages to his chest, then held them out for Rieux to read. The bulk of the manuscript consisted of that first sentence "written again and again with small variants, simplifications or elaborations."

The text still wasn't perfect Grand admitted. But it was too late. He was dying. In a loud, shrill voice he told Grand to "Burn it!"

Ironically, Grand survived. The following morning he told Dr. Rieux "I was overhasty. But I'll make another start. You'll see, I can remember every word."

I thought writing my experiences would be an easy task. All I had to do was record them on tape, have the tapes transcribed, reorganize the material, correct the grammar and submit it for publication. But Grand's struggle became mine as well. As his first efforts were burned, my journal was confiscated before my release. And as the days of my writing turned into weeks, and the weeks into months, I resonated with Joseph Grand's straining to find the words. Like Grand, at times I felt satisfied yet aware that what I was writing had not hit the mark.

As I finish, I remember Grand's final solution to the dilemma of the first sentence of his novel. On inquiry he tells Dr. Rieux that he has indeed made a fresh start. "I've cut out all the adjectives." Then "with a twinkle in his eye, he took his hat off, bringing it low in a courtly sweep."

CHAPTER ONE

LISTEN TO THE CHILDREN

But I say to those who listen, Love your enemies, do good to those who hate you, bless those who curse you, pray for those who abuse you.

—Luke 6:27-28

As I stepped from a car in Rome within days of my release from captivity, a *paparazzi* shouted at me from a distance, "Father Jenco, what are your feelings toward the terrorists who held you?" I responded without much thought: "I'm a Christian. I must forgive them."

Although this was probably the first time I had said so publicly, the sentiment had been in my heart for some time. I had come to understand that my captors could not be my enemies. They had to be my brothers.

Through his life and through his final agony and final words, Jesus taught us that the heart of love is forgiveness. This is what he asked of us. This is what he asked of me during my captivity.

Toward the end of my captivity one of my guards, a man named Sayeed who had at times brutalized me, sat down on my mat with me. He had recently started calling me "Abouna," an Arabic name meaning "dear father." At first I was Jenco, then Lawrence, then Abouna, indicating by the choice of names and tone of voice that a change of heart was taking place. He asked me if I remembered the first six months of my captivity. I responded "Yes, Sayeed. I remember all the pain and suffering

13

you caused me and my brothers." Then he asked "Abouna, do you forgive me?"

These quietly spoken words overwhelmed me. As I sat blindfolded, unable to see the man who had been my enemy, I understood I was called to forgive, to let go of revenge, retaliation, and vindictiveness.

And I was challenged to forgive him unconditionally. I could not forgive him on the condition that he change his behavior to conform to my wishes or values. I had no control over his response. I understood I was to say yes.

I said: "Sayeed, there were times I hated you. I was filled with anger and revenge for what you did to me and my brothers. But Jesus said on a mountain top that I was not to hate you. I was to love you. Sayeed, I need to ask God's forgiveness and yours."

In my frequent prayer during the seemingly endless days of captivity, I reflected on numerous scriptural passages. From Luke (6:36-38) I was told, "Be merciful, just as your Father is merciful. Do not judge, and you will not be judged; do not condemn, and you will not be condemned. Forgive, and you will be forgiven; give, and it will be given to you. A good measure, pressed down, shaken together, running over, will be put into your lap; for the measure you give will be the measure you get back." In the Hebrew Covenant, the sage author, the son of Sirach, wrote (28:2): "Forgive your neighbor the wrong he has done, and then your sins will be pardoned when you pray."

In prayer I go to God asking forgiveness from my sins, and knowing I need to forgive others. If I do not forgive, I cannot be at peace. Mark (11:25) said, "Whenever you stand praying, forgive, if you have anything against anyone; so that your Father in heaven may also forgive you your trespasses." John writes (1 4:20-21) that "Those who say, 'I love God,' and hate their brothers or sisters, are liars; for those who do not love a brother or sister whom they have seen cannot love God whom they have not seen." And in the Sermon on the Mount, Jesus reminded his listeners that if while presenting their offerings before an altar they remembered their brother or sister had something against them, they should first go and be reconciled with their brother or sister.

I wrote these and other passages in my hostage journal. Writing them down was the easy part, making them incarnate was no easy task. Yet I believe God was pushing me hard into an understanding of the commandment of love.

The scene between Sayeed and I depicted two prodigal sons coming together. Sayeed asked for my forgiveness. I asked God and Sayeed to forgive me my anger and hate, my desire to punish and get revenge. This was a graced moment. Two men, alienated brothers, off in our own alien lands, eating the silage of bitterness and resentment, embraced. Two sons came home to their hearts, in which the spirit of peace and reconciliation lives. It was a transforming moment of mutual forgiveness and healing of hurts. The gift of the moment moved us from alienation to reconciliation, and from brokenness to wholeness before God.

When I offered Sayeed my forgiveness, I knew intuitively I had been set free and could go home. I had empowered myself with God's word, "Be kind and tenderhearted to one another and forgive one another as I the God of both of you have forgiven you."

My journey to this challenge of discipleship began, in large measure, with a phone call on July 4, 1984 from Catholic Relief Services (CRS) director Monsignor Robert Charlebois. I was working among the refugees in Thailand at the time and he called to say that CRS would like me to go to Beirut, Lebanon, as program director.

I was not naive about the turmoil in Lebanon or the Middle East, so I asked if I could first visit and get a look at the CRS work there. He said that would be fine.

I arrived in Beirut a few days later and was met by the then current CRS Director Joe Curtin, Sister Madeline Therese, a Holy Cross sister from Notre Dame, Indiana, and other CRS staff members. During the next ten days I learned everything I could about the work of CRS in Lebanon, especially in Beirut.

Its office was in West Beirut, considered the Muslim sector even though many Christians lived there. The diverse origins of the staff reflected, I believe, the fabric of the entire nation. It was a wonderful place, an excellent example of how people from many religious backgrounds can work together for a common cause.

CRS went to Lebanon in 1976 basically as a relief agency to supply food, clothing, and medicine to the people. What developed was an extensive program of reconstructing private institutions such as schools, hospitals, orphanages, homes for the elderly, and the like. One CRS project was a home for former Beirut prostitutes who had lived in makeshift shelters along the burned- and bombed-out area on the "Green Line," a linear park that divided the Muslim (west) and Christian (east) sectors of the city.

CRS also served other groups within the Lebanese community. One project supplied farming equipment. Another established a tailor shop in Tripoli to train women in a trade.

CRS projects were funded not only by CRS monies but also by monies from the Agency for International Development, which were to be used to reconstruct private-sector institutions. The basic thrust of CRS was to solace the poorest of the poor, regardless of religious background. In principle and practice it was completely nondiscriminatory.

The CRS Director Joe Curtin had been in Beirut for several years. Because of the civil war, there was a palpable sense of exhaustion about this man and he clearly needed a break.

Lebanon was a nation torn apart by warring civil factions, its disarray rooted in its French colonial past. When the French left in 1943 they provided the nation with an unwritten agreement called the National Covenant. Its formula called for the division of government among all sects: the Maronite Catholics would provide the president, the Sunni Muslims the Prime Minister, the Shiite Muslims the speaker of parliament, and the Druse Muslims some senior military officers.

In time this national political fabric began to unravel. Internal and external forces caused the fragmentation. Internally, factions in the powerful Maronite Catholic sect were feuding among themselves. They were at enmity with the Druse, a mysterious sect of Islam founded around the eleventh century.

The demographics were shifting in favor of the Shiite Muslims, a shift caused by a number of factors: rapid population growth, a truthful census, and the exodus of Christians and Sunnis from Lebanon. The Shiite community of mostly poor laborers from southern Lebanon and the Bekaa Valley became the unofficial but factual majority. Oppressed and exploited, they clamored for greater voice in the politics of the nation and a more equitable share in the nation's wealth for housing, health care, education, and jobs.

They were further motivated to challenge the power elites by the success of their Iranian brothers' and sisters' revolution in Iran, who also provided financial and spiritual support.

External forces pressuring the nation included Israel's occupation of a large segment in the south; the presence of the Palestinian refugees who, expelled from London in 1970, had settled in Lebanon; the border conflicts between the Palestinians and the Israelis; and the constant interference by other Middle Eastern nations in Lebanon's internal affairs.

When Israel invaded Lebanon in 1978 and again in 1982, the Shiites became refugees in their own nation—fleeing from south Lebanon to the southern suburbs of Beirut. Such events created the atmosphere for a once exploited, oppressed, and passive minority to explode as a radical fundamentalist majority. From this community a group of radical men and women formed the *Islamic Jihad*—Islamic Holy War. They came under the umbrella of Hezbollah, the Iranian-founded Party of God.

At the time I considered the job, however, peace initiatives appeared to have taken root. The Green Line had been opened, the government was convening again and trying to restore order. It looked as if the years of civil war were coming to an end. It seemed a fortuitous moment to bring in a successor at CRS.

During those days, I met with Christian religious leaders—Roman, Maronite, Armenian, Syrian, and Greek Catholics,

Orthodox prelates, and Protestant clergy—and with Muslim spiritual leaders—Sunni, Shiite, and Druze. I agreed to become Program Director of CRS.

But first I returned to Bangkok to collect my belongings and say goodbye. Then I visited my home in Joliet, Illinois, where I celebrated the twenty-fifth anniversary of my ordination as a priest.

I was back in Beirut on October 1 and moved into Joe Curtin's apartment in order to use the remaining months on his lease. During the three months I had been away, the situation in Lebanon had deteriorated completely. Every evening, with the setting of the sun, the warring militia attacked each other and wrought tremendous violence on Beirut, indeed upon the whole country.

Sometimes the violence was so horrendous I would throw my bedding onto the living room floor and lie there awake all night, hoping that the wall between the bedroom and living room would provide some protection against the mortars, bombs, shrapnel, and bullets flying outside. Once I got up in the middle of the night and wrote in large black calligraphy on the wall, "Dear God, I will to live."

As Christmas approached, it was suggested that I go to East Beirut to celebrate, and arrangements were made for me to offer Mass at the home of a Maronite Catholic family.

I arrived at their home on Christmas Eve directly after visiting a Palestinian refugee camp where there was tremendous poverty and suffering. The contrast couldn't have been more striking. Here was Papa Noel dressed in his Santa Claus costume passing out gifts to the children beside a beautiful Christmas tree. A table was laden with food and three or four Sri Lankan servants waited on us.

Because of this contrast I decided not to preach on the gospel narratives about the infant Jesus. It's so easy, so safe, to approach God as an infant in a manger. But our faith is very costly and our faith is an adult faith. So I took as the subject of my Christmas homily a sermon the Lord Jesus gave on a mountain top, the Gospel according to Matthew, chapters 5-7.

At the Kiss of Peace I said "Shalom" on this night of the birth of the Servant of Peace, a Jew whose name is Jesus. At the end of Mass though, I was rebuked by the head of the house, a woman who spoke English with a heavy French accent. She said to me, "Where, American, do you get the right to use a Jewish word in our home?" And she went on about the suffering that Christians had been through at the hands of Jews.

Later I sat on the floor and wondered if we pass on our hatred to our children. The little ones came and sat all around me. I looked into their beautiful brown eyes and asked them, "What is your world all about?" As the adults listened, these children spoke to me about a world of peace. One child said something truly astonishing, "I can't even pray unless I forgive." I looked at the adults and said, "Do you ever listen to your children?" Their response was strange. The middle-aged people, like the lady who challenged me for using the word "shalom," remained tight-lipped. But several of the older ones asked to go to confession.

This night for celebrating the birth of Jesus was punctuated by tremendous violence. Outside the Muslim militia were retaliating against the Christians for what they had done the day before, that is, bombed the Muslims. How little we've learned in these two thousand years, I thought. We're even ignorant of what these little children know.

On January 7, the day after Epiphany, I was not feeling very well. My father died at fifty-three of a massive heart attack. I thought perhaps I might have inherited his predisposition, so I decided to have it checked out. When I arrived at my office, I asked Sr. Madeline Therese to recommend a good doctor. She sent me to someone whose office was just up the street from CRS.

That morning, the doctor performed a series of tests, including blood work. He then recommended I not return to work. I went back to the office briefly, but only to let my staff know I was taking time to rest and would be at home.

That evening the doctor called to tell me he wanted to run some more tests so we made an appointment for the next morning, Tuesday, January 8.

Tuesday I rose early, celebrated Mass as I normally did, then prepared breakfast. My driver was due at 7:30 a.m. Drivers were common for security reasons. They knew their way around and could avoid unsafe areas. And they knew how to drive well should problems occur. The day held my appointment with the doctor and a signature ceremony at the Lebanese government offices—part of the process of disbursing monies to the institutions designated within CRS mandates.

I left my apartment that morning carrying a few things I'd brought home from the office the day before. Around my neck was a silver chain and cross I treasured, a gift from an Australian Servite brother for my twenty-fifth anniversary of ordination.

My driver pulled up at about 7:30 for a trip to CRS that normally took about a quarter of an hour. I was in the car only a few minutes.

We turned a corner in a very congested area of the Hamra district of West Beirut where many Westerners worked and where the American University was located, then stopped at an intersection. Parents were either walking or driving their children to school. The owner of the neighborhood grocery store was directing traffic. At the corner four policemen stood talking.

I turned to my driver and said, "Khaled, isn't that strange? The policemen are standing on the corner talking while a grocer in a white apron directs traffic."

Within seconds a tremendous crash of automatic weapons fire shattered the morning. I looked up and saw men rushing the car, guns shooting wildly toward the heavens. I heard another explosion behind us. I turned around to see more men firing weapons skyward. People all around were fleeing, terrified.

"Khaled," I said turning to him, "I'm going to be kidnapped."

Two men yanked us from the front of the car and shoved us into its back seat, pushed in next to us and slammed the rear doors. Three others climbed into the front. Khaled said to me, "Abouna, don't worry! It will only be a couple moments and they will let us go." One of the men in front ripped out a side compartment containing the car documents. I thought, "How strange to damage a car like this. All he had to do was open the compartment." The four policemen had vanished.

Because of the shooting the street was completely empty. My captors drove down a hill and turned onto a road along the Corniche, a broad avenue along the sea, to an area not far from the Hamra district. We parked adjacent to a mosque. They hustled us out of the car, locked Khaled in its trunk, and forced me into a second car pushing me down onto the floor. They then drove for a while before stopping. I heard planes and knew we were someplace near the airport in the city's southern suburbs. They waited awhile. Then they transferred me from the floor of the car to the trunk. As I was thrown into the trunk, the silver cross and chain fell out from beneath my collar. One of the guards saw it and took it from me. I never saw it again.

CHAPTER TWO

MISTAKEN IDENTITY

Not everyone in chains is subdued; at times, a chain is greater than a necklace.
                                        —Kahill Gibran

In the darkness of the car trunk, my first thoughts were of Father Jerzy Popieluszko who also had been thrown into a trunk. A parish priest in suburban Warsaw, he spoke out against abuses of the Polish Communist government and supported the then-banned Solidarity movement. He was abducted by the Polish secret police on October 19, 1984, his savagely beaten body found eleven days later in an icy reservoir.

I also thought of the different stages one supposedly goes through on realizing that death is imminent—denial, anger, bargaining, depression, and acceptance. I prayed, "Listen, God, I don't have the luxury of going through all those stages now. I need to quickly accept my own dying now!"

I always expected that when facing my death, I would be consumed by a sense of my sinfulness before God and of my need for forgiveness. I was surprised that my mind didn't flash to an Act of Contrition. Instead, I found a sense of peace, believing it was better to trust in God's mercy, gentleness, and compassion. I found myself praying how beautiful God is in the works of creation.

They drove to another isolated spot in the suburbs of southern Beirut overlooking the Mediterranean Sea and waited for a while.

Then they transferred me to the trunk of an old junker. I remembered they used such cars as bombs. They would pack them with explosives, park them next to targeted buildings, and detonate them. Sometimes it would destroy the building; usually it would kill any number of innocent men, women, and children. I thought, "So this is how I am to die—in the trunk of a car used as a bomb."

We waited for about an hour. My body ached in the fetal position required in the trunk. I tried to move to help relieve the pain of leg cramps. A small hole let in some light and I tried to adjust my body to that hole, hoping to see outside. The guards could tell I was moving and banged on the trunk top.

They started the car and as we drove away I finally positioned my face near the hole. I could see little at that angle. The road was paved—my only luxury. Shortly, we turned left into an alleyway.

They stopped, opened the trunk, pulled me out, and rushed me into a one-story building that appeared to be under construction. They brought me to an unfinished bathroom with a dirt floor and an old bathtub in the corner. They stripped me to my shirt and sat me down on a cement block. Several well-dressed people who spoke English very well came in to interrogate me.

"Are you Mr. Joseph Curtin?"

"No, I'm not Joseph Curtin. I'm Father Jenco."

After asking me this a number of times it dawned on me: they had kidnapped the wrong man! I believed they would set me free as soon as they realized their mistake. I told them I had a doctor's appointment that afternoon, but they did not respond. I was not particularly worried because it was all a mistake and I thought they'd let me go because I was a priest.

Around 4:30 p.m. the January sun was beginning to set and I was very cold. I turned around to look into the eyes of a young man standing guard over me. I saw the eyes of hate.

"You are dead," he said.

"Why?" I asked.

No response.

Around 9:30 p.m. my captors brought me into the living room of a Muslim family and bedded me down. To keep me from listening to their conversation they put a headset over my ears. All I could hear was Arabic music from a cassette player. They brought me a cola and a hamburger, but I wasn't hungry and I didn't eat. With a pounding headache I slept fitfully.

Early in the next morning they woke me and let me go to the toilet. When I came out, they put an old sweater on my head, pulled it down over my eyes, and began to wind tape around my head down to the tip of my nose.

I thought, "Oh, I know what. Following the Arabic tradition of saving face, they're going to make it look as if I had an accident and just dump me off at some hospital nearby."

A few minutes later, I was back in a car trunk. We arrived next at a garage where they took me out of the trunk. I couldn't see anything, but I could hear people talking and pounding some boards. My hopes about Arab face-saving dwindled with the thought that they were constructing my coffin.

A voice said to stand up and "put your arms to your sides and your ankles and legs as close as you can get them." Then they wound wide packing tape around my ankles, legs, torso, shoulders, and neck. When they came to my head they said "Open your mouth," stuffed a piece of cloth inside, and taped my mouth shut. They wound the tape around my head. My whole body was wrapped with only my nostrils left exposed for breathing.

Then they slid me under the bed of a truck into the space where tires are usually stored. I heard a metal door close, but didn't know where they had put me. I thought they had wrapped my body for burial and put me in a hearse.

I rode in this hot metal box. It was burning, the exhaust fumes so sickening and overpowering I could hardly breathe. Nor, bound as I was, could I brace myself in any way. The truck hit a bump so hard that I flew up and hit my nose. It bled and the blood coagulated in my nasal passages making it even harder to breathe. The truck stopped several times but the engine kept running. I figured we were stopping at checkpoints and I hoped maybe the guards would find me. I was afraid and started to pray.

I remembered the Jesus prayer of the Russian mystics and desert fathers. Breathing in and out I prayed, "Lord Jesus, Son of God, have mercy on me, a sinner." With every difficult breath, "Lord Jesus, Son of God, have mercy on me, a sinner." Breathing Jesus in and out, in and out through the drying blood in my nose. Slowly, gradually, with the rhythm of my breathing, a feeling of peace came over me. For hours the prayer controlled my panic of suffocation. Finally the truck came to a halt and the engine went silent.

I was pretty much out of it, near asphyxiation. They pulled me out from under the truck and dumped me, limp and dazed, nearby. But the cool air was refreshing. I wondered what would be next: torture? death? The questions came: Where am I? What's happening at the CRS office? Does my family know I've been kidnapped? There were no answers and I felt powerless.

They grabbed me again and lifted me off the ground. I sensed I was inside and that they were lugging me up stairs. We went up and then turned—up and turning—four times before they dumped me again. When they cut the tape from my body and pulled the gag from my mouth, my first words were in Latin: *"Resurrexit, sicut dixit, alleluia, alleluia."* "He is risen as he said, alleluia, alleluia."

I was in the first of many prisons. I took off my sweater-blindfold making eye-to-eye contact with two startled guards. Returning my look one of them said, "You must wear the blindfold. When anyone comes into this building, you must have the blindfold on." I understood this to mean that I did not have to wear it in their presence, only in the presence of people other than the guards and when going to and from the toilet. I would find out later that I was to see no one, not even the guards. If I did, they told me, "you are dead."

But the sweater was loose-knit enough that I could see

through it. I feigned non-sight when it covered my eyes though I could see everywhere and everyone.

They took me to their sleeping quarters and made me sit facing the wall. Catching the eye of one young guard I let him know I was hungry. He went to the kitchen, opened a can of green beans, a can of tomato sauce, put a little water in a pan, mixed them all together, and returned with my meal. Hostage cuisine. I was hungry and it was delicious.

In the afternoon they moved me into a corridor and chained me to a radiator outside the bathroom. They laid out a mat for me to sleep on. Later they moved me again, this time to the kitchen where they chained me to another radiator. When they let me go to the bathroom I could stand on the toilet, look out the window and see the ancient Roman ruins of Baalbek. We were somewhere in the mountains overlooking the Bekaa Valley.

I could also stand up and look out the kitchen window. Through the spaces in a decorative cement block wall I saw that it was snowing. I also saw birds flying in and out of the trees. But I was a hostage chained to a radiator! "If I could just get free of this chain!" I thought. Maybe I could kick out some of those blocks, enough to squeeze through, and flee this kitchen prison to some sanctuary. In the distance, I heard church bells.

CHAPTER THREE

SOMEWHERE OVER THE RAINBOW

They tell me: if you see a slave sleeping, do not wake him lest he be dreaming of freedom. I tell them: if you see a slave sleeping, wake him and explain to him of freedom.
—Kahill Gibran

An old Jewish proverb says what a person in a situation like mine does. "The first thing one does is cry. The second thing one does is sing. And the third thing one does is become silent." I found this saying to be true.

Confined alone in my kitchen prison, I cried out of sheer loneliness. Then I looked out the window and saw the birds in their freedom and started to sing: "Somewhere over the rainbow . . .," a song with special poignancy for me. As one of the young, newly-ordained Servite priests in Rome twenty-six years earlier it had been sung to us by the student choir from the Servite college. And in isolation, silence was my constant companion. Rarely could I talk with anyone or would anyone talk to me. The young guards would appear each morning, fix breakfast, and disappear. I would pass the time in different ways, keeping track of the days by using my saliva to mark in the dust of the tile walls with my finger.

I was still wearing the clothes I had on when kidnapped— a white shirt and a gray sweater and pants. They also gave me a t-shirt and a pair of shorts. The radiator I was chained to was adjacent to the sink so I could wash my clothes and drape them over the radiator to dry. I could have clean clothes every day, if I wanted to.

The kitchen floor was filthy, so I took a rag and stretching out my chain, wiped the floor around my mat as far as I could reach. I could also stretch out and knock a few potatoes from a sack in the corner. I'd eat them raw. In the same corner sat a box of neglected, rotting fruit. I'd get a piece of the fruit and throw it out to the birds. Or I'd watch my companions—some ants who regularly came foraging in my quarters—and I'd put a little food by their hole.

Since the guards would only permit one trip to the toilet per day, I came to appreciate the proximity of the sink. When I needed to urinate—and the guards never knew this—I would relieve myself into a jar, pour it down the sink, and flush it with water.

On that once-a-day trip to the bathroom, I was permitted a hot shower. But one day there was an explosion in the basement. The furnace was destroyed and we no longer had heat in the building. After that the guards piled lots of blankets on me for warmth at night. And when I washed my clothes it would take much longer for them to dry. Relatively speaking, I liked that prison. At least I could look out the window.

I didn't have a Bible, but from day one of my captivity I would recall God's word unveiled to me in Christian and Hebrew covenants. Knowing the eucharistic prayer by heart, I'd take some Arabic bread and celebrate eucharist. I'd retain a piece of the eucharistic Christ and when I was sad, lonely, confused, or bored, I would hold onto the Christ.

From pieces of string off the potato sack, I fashioned a rosary and created my own versions of the joyful, sorrowful, and glorious mysteries. Sometimes I'd focus on the persons of holy scripture as I prayed—on Mary, or Joseph, or the apostles.

Once a young guard saw me praying my string rosary. He gave me a precious gift from around his neck—a string of Muslim prayer beads.

It contained thirty-three beads. It's prayed by holding a

bead between thumb and forefinger and giving God a name. You progress from bead to bead giving God a different name with each bead. Then you go around two more times until you have prayed a total of ninety-nine names for God. I used these beads in exactly this manner. I was amazed at how many names I came up with, without even knowing any names used by Muslims. I wore these prayer beads around my neck throughout my captivity and wanted to keep them, but my captors took them back when I was released.

During these days I also formulated my own litany of saints. I included the familiar ones of the Roman canon and I remembered many people in my life whom I believe are present to God's eternal love and grace: my mother and father, an aunt, an uncle, a grandmother, a relative, a friend, a Servite . . .

Steve Nichols was one of these many saints. He had been my director when I worked for CRS in the Yemen Arab Republic from 1981 to 1983. A week before he was to be married, he was killed while jogging along a Red Sea beach in Hodeida. He was hit by a young man driving home in his family car.

I absolutely love Steve and, believing as I do that he is present to God, I would pray, "Steve, ask God to set me free."

Another of my saints was Andy Colletti, a Servite who suffered greatly his entire life. I was Andy's superior when he died and had tremendous reverence for him in all his great sufferings. I believe that he, too, is present to an eternal embrace of love.

When I was first bound with tape, I put my glasses in a pants pocket and prayed they wouldn't break because I can't see without them. Fortunately they didn't because the guards gave me a couple of books. One was a cheap novel about a huge Australian snake. I wished I hadn't read it because it gave me nightmares. Another one was an abridged version of Charles Dickens' *David Copperfield*, which I reread about a thousand times.

They also brought in a television and video tape player and let me watch the movie Barabbas with them. Afterward, they asked me question after question about Barabbas, whom they

liked and thought of as a great saint and liberator. I told them
what I knew, which wasn't much, including the scriptural passages in which he is mentioned. To create the film was more an
act of creative mythology than history. But they seemed to
receive it as if it were a docu-drama or a re-enactment.

In time I realized other captives were being held in this
apartment. I could hear voices, including a woman's, and
watched the guards preparing food in the kitchen. They would
put six plates, including mine, on the floor and fill them, so I
assumed there must be five other prisoners.

I didn't know who they were. In fact, names like Ben Weir,
William Buckley, and Jerry Levin—those kidnapped before me—
hadn't found much place in my understanding yet. I suppose
most Americans wouldn't have recognized their names either.
The media hadn't provided much coverage of their kidnappings
at that point.

My two young guards were rather pleasant men, although
their English wasn't the greatest. This made for occasional light
moments. One day, one of them told me a story about his sister's
vacation in Europe. In a restaurant in Switzerland she wanted to
order chicken, but didn't know the word for chicken in either
French, Italian, or German. So she tried to demonstrate to the
waiter what she wanted by clucking and flapping her arms like a
chicken, which made everyone in the restaurant break up in fits
of laughter. As my young guard told the story he himself started
laughing and it became rather contagious. Hearing the story in
the guard's fractured English made it even funnier. I believe our
laughter and smiles helped change attitudes: enemies were
becoming friends.

Sometimes one of my young guards would come to my
kitchen cell and hand me a little bag of cookies, and tell me they
were from his wife. I suspect that they had an apartment in this
same building.

And then one day Hajj, the man who had me kidnapped,
paid me a visit. I only discovered later who he was: at this point
I didn't even know why I had been kidnapped.

My kidnappers were Shiites, a fundamentalist Muslim sect, who believed that western influences were corrupting the Middle East. They were a minority that wanted Lebanon to be an Islamic state. The brother of Hajj's wife had been convicted of bombing the American and French embassies in Beirut and was in jail. Hajj wanted a hostage to exchange for his brother-in-law and went after Joe Curtin but took me by mistake.

I hardly ever wore my blindfold, but since they insisted that I wear it whenever someone came into the room, I put the old sweater over my head when Hajj came in. He then spoke to me through an interpreter. It was just a very simple conversation in which he told me that I would be going home soon.

Soon. That word would become very, very difficult for me. As the days became weeks and the weeks turned into months, then a year, I didn't want to hear what became an empty word. Strange to imagine that one syllable could be so painful.

One night I noticed a rat running around my room. Since I slept on the floor I just didn't appreciate it. Well, I found myself in a position similar to the guard's sister trying to order chicken in a Swiss restaurant. I had to imitate a rat running around the room. The guard caught on and I was able to persuade him to close the door to their bathroom that was just off the kitchen.

The guards would leave the light on in the kitchen at all hours, which made it really difficult for me to sleep. But I discovered I could turn it off by extending my chain as far as possible and flipping the switch with a broom handle. Sometimes I woke up early in the morning and made tea. My chain was long enough that I could get water from the sink, boil it in a pot on the small two-plate gas burner, and make tea without them knowing it. But they caught me one morning and, apparently displeased, stashed the tea in a place I couldn't reach.

They also stored a bottle of wine vinegar out of my reach, which seemed strange to me. Moslems are not supposed to drink alcoholic beverages, but my guards would take a shot now and then the way some people take a shot of whiskey.

One night my guards were watching television in their room

and one of them came into the kitchen to make popcorn. I think it must have been the first time he'd ever tried. I'm a popcorn freak and watched his every move. He put in the oil, and then the popcorn, but he didn't put a lid on the pan. I thought, "He is going to put a lid on that pan, I know he is." But he didn't. Suddenly the kernels were exploding and popcorn was flying all over the room. When he realized he needed a lid he couldn't find one so he frantically grabbed half a dozen things before deciding on a plate. He managed to salvage some, though.

And then it happened, what I had hardly dared to hope for: he offered me some. I can't even begin to describe how I felt at that moment, except to say that I could've cried. Then, when he brought it to me, and my eyes gazed on the charred product, I did cry. Oh, yes I ate some. I was just so hungry.

There was an Iranian military camp nearby (Syria was aligned with Iran and together they controlled the Bekaa Valley), and every day around noon I could look out the window and see Iranian soldiers in jeeps coming down the hill bringing food for the hostages as well as the guards.

I'd hear a lot of commotion and horns blowing outside and soon guards would come up the stairs with big containers of food—usually mutton, potatoes, and tomatoes. It was rather tasty and warm. In such times when they gave me an abundance of food, I would stash it like a little squirrel, especially the bread.

Early on February 14, a month and six days after I was kidnapped, I saw the guards outside running around pointing up to the building. Carrying their automatic weapons, they were very agitated and angry. They came up the stairs and I wondered what was going on. They wanted me to go to the bathroom. I had to wear my sweater-blindfold, so I took off my glasses and left them next to the radiator with my white shirt and gray pants and sweater.

When I came out of the bathroom, they took me to a bedroom, empty except for a foam mattress on the floor. Through the weave in the sweater, I saw two blankets tied together lying on the mattress and knew what the commotion was about: a prisoner had escaped. He used the blankets to let himself out his window.

They sat me down on the mat and I looked around the room. It was sealed, the windows now shuttered. I wouldn't be able to look out and I thought, "Oh, I hope they don't want me to stay here." I wanted to go back to my kitchen prison where I could get a glass of water when I wanted, or use the sink as a urinal, or steal and hoard food, or watch who came and who went.

A guard brought me a glass with a pencil standing in it. I had no idea why he gave me the pencil but I took it and wrote on the wall, "Today is February 14, the Feast of St. Valentine."

A couple of anxious hours passed. I did not like having been moved. Even in prison the familiar provides a sense of safety and security. The guards returned, gave me my gray pants, white shirt, and gray sweater, and told me to dress. Then they blindfolded me, took me downstairs and out the door to a garage. Through my blindfold I saw a car with the trunk open. They spread a blanket on the floor of the trunk and told me to climb in. I was not bound and they covered me with another blanket, telling me to make myself comfortable. The trunk slammed. Darkness again.

Again I thought they were going to kill me because of their harsh pushing and shoving. After driving for a short period they stopped and took me out of the car into a garage with stalls erected in it. The walls were steel sheeting and the roofs, wire mesh.

They sat me down on a dusty mat in one of these stalls. After the guards left I lifted my blindfold and saw a pair of shoes, covered with dust, at the end of the mat. I wondered whom they belonged to and if the person who lived there before me was still alive. Cheerful thoughts.

I was very cold because my clothes were inadequate for the temperature of the garage. As I sat on the mat I thought about the times I plotted escape from my previous prison. The bathroom window there was covered with a sheet of self-adhesive plastic which was supposed to look like stained glass. I had scratched a hole in it and would peek through and see the ruins of Baalbek. Having heard church bells in the distance, I thought that if I managed to escape, I could find sanctuary in that church. But these stalls? It was pretty hopeless.

A couple hours passed and the guards came to move me again. They put me into the trunk of the same car and soon we were driving even higher into the mountains. Finally we stopped. They opened the trunk to let me out. Through my blindfold I saw a one-story residential building under construction. They took me into a living room with an oil heater in the center. I heard voices speaking both Arabic and English and thought I must have been with other hostages. They were being questioned.

A young, wiry, and very agitated guard stuck the end of his automatic weapon under my blindfold as if he was about to kill me. Furious, he demanded information about people living in Lebanon, especially in Beirut. He told me to read what the man next to me wrote and to say whether it was true or not. I wanted to know who the man was—I was not aware that it was Ben Weir—but I was not the one asking the questions.

I had left my glasses in the kitchen when they had first moved me to the escaped hostage's room and now to here. I told the guard, "I cannot read without my glasses. My glasses are on the kitchen floor." My anxiety in this situation was becoming unbearable. I thought I would now be in captivity without my glasses. I pleaded with them, "Someone please get my glasses for me." But they paid no attention.

This same agitated guard then faced me toward the wall, took off my blindfold and gave me pen and paper. He demanded I write the names of Americans living in Beirut, telling him who were Democrats and Republicans. I told him I didn't know these things, that I had been in Lebanon only from October to January and had not met many people. Most Americans had left the country by then and I never asked people if they were Democrat or Republican. We just didn't ask those kinds of questions. Since he got no information, he was very angry with me.

They put my sweater-blindfold back over my eyes but evidently had no idea I could see everyone in the room through its loose weave. They were seated around the heater—young men, all bearing arms of some sort. The wiry character seemed to be in charge. Only one of the guards from the previous prison was there. What a drastic change!

It was evening, about six or seven o'clock. A man came into the room, mixed a drink of some sort and gave it to me. I drank it not realizing it was a drug. Then they walked me to a car and loaded me into the back seat. I was seated next to one of my original guards. We drove away and from the switchbacks and changing altitude it felt like we were going higher into the mountains. The drug was potent and I fell asleep, my head on the guard's shoulder. He adjusted his position, cradling me.

When we stopped I was hardly conscious of being walked into another building. There were building cubicles within. In my stupor, everything was so strange. I couldn't quite hold onto reality. I felt as if I was leaving my body, as if I was somewhere else. I started to say something and in the middle of it my mind went to a place of no words. My mind seemed very free for a while, but then something happened. It seemed as if I was suddenly waking from a very vivid dream, slammed into the sights, sounds, and smells again—indeed, into the pain again—of my captivity.

That night I fell asleep between two guards in a room full of people—captive and free—but all hostages, prisoners in one way or another.

Morning came, and groggy, I tried to focus my eyes. After a while we were led to our little cubicles. That night in the darkness a voice to my right asked, "Who are you?" Before I could answer a voice to my left replied, "I am Ben Weir. I'm a Presbyterian minister." Then I said, "I am Father Lawrence Martin Jenco. I'm the director of Catholic Relief Services." Then the man who asked the question said, "I am William Buckley. I am an American diplomat from the embassy in Beirut." I did not get to meet this man face to face, or get to know him, though I was in the same prison with him when he died.

I also learned that the man who escaped was a journalist named Jerry Levin and that a Saudi man and woman were in with us. I knew nothing about the Saudis except that the woman cried a lot. Our walls were pressed cardboard and we could all hear any of us breathing.

This mountain prison, a primitive house, was so cold that urine would freeze. Water was at a premium. From February 14 to March 15 we were not allowed to wash. The toilet leaked through the ceiling above us and water gathered on the dirt floor in puddles, which I used to wash my hands if it didn't freeze. There was no toilet paper. There was nothing. We just had to endure.

On February 17, Hajj paid a visit. I knelt on the floor in front of Ben Weir where I couldn't see him and wrote my first letter as a hostage. Ben translated what Hajj was saying in Arabic— what I must write and to whom.

I was told to write to my family and a major cleric in the United States. I thought of writing the Bishop of Joliet, but abandoned that notion out of simple embarrassment at not remembering how to spell his name. I remembered that my boss in New York, Monsignor Robert Charlebois, was a friend of Cardinal Joseph Bernardin of Chicago. So I wrote a letter to him and one to my brothers and sisters. Ben repeated what I was to write:

Dear Cardinal Joseph Bernardin,

I, Father Lawrence Jenco, Director of Catholic Relief in Lebanon, am being held hostage for those men being held hostage in Kuwait. As long as they are held I am held.

Any military intervention on my behalf will not be good for me.

In ☧,

Fr. Lawrence M. Jenco

In the letter to my family I was instructed to tell them I would be *hanged* if the U.S. attempted a rescue. It was terrible to write the word "hanged." I found myself speaking to God in my heart, "Oh God, I prefer being shot." Then I asked Ben, "The correct English, is it 'hanged' or is it 'hung'? I don't remember."

Odd. In the shadow of the gallows I was thinking, as if I'd been granted a final request, "Yes, actually, my preferred manner of execution is the firing squad; but if you insist on the noose, please grant me the courtesy of a dictionary: I deserve to know whether I'm being hanged or being hung." But, I confess, it really only became humorous in retrospect.

They provided a nondescript envelope, which I addressed to my sister, Mae Mihelich, in Joliet. When I gave it to my captors, I wondered if they were really going to mail it, and, if they did, whether it would ever reach its destination. What if it were intercepted by some agency of the U.S. government, or if it were simply lost?

But for many, many miles, this common envelope belied its extraordinary contents. One morning it simply arrived at my sister's home in a routine delivery of ordinary mail. My nephew brought it in saying "Look, Mom, a letter from Uncle Larry."

It arrived as my family was creating a plan of action on my behalf. They had learned of the kidnapping from the early morning news reports on January 8. Within a few hours, brothers, sisters, nieces, and nephews had gathered at my sister Mae's home to deal with the media.

At first they had been at a loss on what to do. But they soon planned to meet every Monday night to say the rosary and plan activities for the upcoming week. They chose a nephew, Andrew Mihelich, to be chairperson. All decisions were consensus.

In the course of nineteen months they travelled to Washington, D.C. to enlist the help of congressmen and senators and to meet with President Reagan and other cabinet and State Department officials. Mae and my other sister, Sue Franceschini, were the principal spokespersons and travelled to many cities to speak on my behalf.

Other relatives and friends tied into the Jenco network trying to make people aware of the American hostages in Beirut.

Other families of hostages came together as a unified front to pressure the American government to secure our release. They also secured the assistance of Catholic and Protestant clerics.

My family did bring my letter addressed to Cardinal Bernardin to him and he said that he and the Archdiocese of Chicago would pray for my release.

CHAPTER FOUR

LOVE REIGNS INVISIBLY

Let me love you, my Lord and my God, and see myself as I really am: a pilgrim in this world, a Christian called to respect and love all whose lives I touch . . . my friends and my enemies.

—Pope Clement XI

For nearly six months I was held in virtual solitary confinement except when the guards decided to abuse me. I kept track of time by tying a knot in a potato sack string for each day, a larger knot to indicate the end of a week. As the months passed, I doubled the size of the larger knot to indicate the end of a month.

Although within earshot of other hostages—I could hear them speak to the guards—I didn't have the opportunity to look into their eyes or learn much about them. Sometimes, unknown to the guards, we would speak with one another; or for one reason or another, we were brought into each other's presence.

In my little cubicle the boring existence of my days passed, knot by knot. This place, high in the mountains (my second prison), was frigid cold, so they would occasionally bring in a hot air blower to warm our cubicles. But they'd turn it on and leave it on, and it became so hot I couldn't breathe. One day I tried to move the thing, and the guards became angry. I felt frustrated having to explain to them why I needed to move the blower.

We were chained here, left hand and left foot, and our chains stretched into the guards' living quarters so they were aware of any movement we made. It wasn't the comforts of home, or, for that matter, even the comforts of my first quarters as a hostage.

Late one March morning none of the guards showed up. I hadn't used the toilet since the previous morning and I simply couldn't bear the pain any longer. So I urinated at the end of my bed into the mattress so the urine would be absorbed and not run along the floor or into another cubicle. Then Ben Weir peeked around the wall that separated our cubicles and said to me, "I think the place is laced with bombs and they've left and they're going to blow us up and kill us." Then he disappeared. Since he had the end cubicle, one of his walls was the wall of the building itself, which had a small window overhead from which one could see the valley below. Thinking we were alone, he stood up on his mat and opened the window. Seeing someone in the distance, he started yelling for help in Arabic.

Well, we hadn't been left alone. Ben's shouting woke the young guard who came flying into the room while Ben was still shouting for help. The guard threw him to the floor and kicked him repeatedly. He was brutal to him, and even chained him differently, with his hands behind his back, telling him that he was going to be killed. They also stopped giving him food.

Ben Weir was such a kind and generous man. During this time the guards hadn't been giving me any water, but Ben would push his water bottle around the partition and share his water with me. Mutual support helped to keep us alive in more ways than one.

Why they wouldn't give me any water I'll never know. Water was a major, conscious, ongoing concern of my daily life—when, where, and how I would get to drink it: when, where, and how I'd get to eliminate it; when I'd get to wash and how I'd get dry.

After breakfast I was allowed to go to the toilet, and that was my only opportunity to get water. When I went to the bathroom I'd wash my face and dry it with my clothes since there were no towels, and I would drink as much water as I possibly could hold. But this meant I would have difficulties later since I could not use the toilet again and was not given a urine bottle.

On one occasion while I was being held in a clothes closet, the guards gave me a can of cola. After I drank it, I kept the empty can hoping to use it as a urinal. Trying to urinate into the small hole at the top of this can with one hand and foot chained was almost impossible in my darkened closet cell. But I didn't get to try for long. The guards caught me and angrily took the can away.

On the morning of March 15, the guards bring me into their living quarters. I'm going to be moved again. Mr. Buckley will go as well. A better place, a better prison I hope.

They tell me to stand with my feet as close together as possible, and start taping me up like a mummy again. The guard winds the tape to my jaw and stops:

"Open your mouth!" he says, preparing to shove a cloth gag in.

"I cannot breathe when you do that," I reply.

Then he swings his hands, clubbing me on both sides of my head. Taped and blindfolded, I don't see the blows coming, and can't even duck or lean to cushion the blow. It hurts and I cry out. He jams the gag into my mouth and tells me to shut up. A couple of them carry me out and dump me in a car trunk. I lay in the trunk expecting the lid to slam. But I sense someone lean in toward me. Suddenly the tape is ripped away from my mouth, the gag pulled out, and the tape replaced. Then the trunk lid slams shut.

As we drive away I wonder who would do this, and figure perhaps it is one of my original guards, since they had been kinder than the current group.

We arrive somewhere and the engine stops. I hear footsteps approaching the trunk. The trunk opens and I notice in the renewal of light that my head hasn't been taped well enough to completely block my vision. I get hauled out of the trunk. We're in a garage. I look eyeball to eyeball at the guards' faces and they don't know it. One man has a very young face—blue eyes and red hair. How strange to look into his eyes! Some of them start to apply a putty-like substance to my body. I hear them laugh, saying in English they can blow me up from the cabin of the truck they are about to transport me in if I make any noise. I get it that this putty is some kind of explosive. They're trying to scare me as they laugh and tell me to touch it which, of course, I can't do. They tell me to look at it, which they think I can't do. But I am looking at it pretty hard through the cracks in my blindfold. Then in their laughter one of them whispers in English, "It's a dud." They think this is about the funniest thing they've ever heard. Mockery is fun. It's all a joke. But I'm not laughing.

Once again they lift me up, and this time I can see what they're doing as they try to slide me into the tire storage area in the underbelly of the truck. To make the process easier, and, I suppose, to provide a cushion for me, they put a blanket underneath me. But there's not enough space, so they pull it out and just slide my body along the steel bed. I'm pretty well concealed.

Having survived one trip already beneath a truck, I steel myself for the trip to the next prison. The Jesus prayer, the inhaling and exhaling of the words, "Lord Jesus Christ, Son of God, have mercy on me!" calms me. A few hours later I hear traffic, people talking, and the sound of airplanes landing and taking off. I am back in the southern suburbs of Beirut.

They had moved me to my third prison. My expectations of a better place were shattered when they put me in a 3' x 6' clothes closet in the guards' room. They blindfolded me by putting a black plastic bag over my head and chained my left hand and foot. I lifted the plastic bag and, through a crack between door and doorjamb, I saw a man chained to a bed. Later I found out it was Terry Anderson.

I hadn't washed in the month since I was moved from my kitchen prison and it was really hot in my new "improved" cell. The guards would cook in their room and keep the heaters going making the closet very warm. When I opened the closet door more than a crack trying to get some circulation, they'd slam it shut. Later they hung a plastic shower curtain, decorated with pink flamingos, over the doorway. I must have counted those flamingos a thousand times. The curtain cut off the air circulation as effectively as closing the door. If I tried to push the curtain aside, the guards became very angry. They apparently thought that I was eyeing them. I just wanted to keep from suffocating. Ironically, with the curtain shut I could see the guards perfectly. At first they didn't realize that, but later they caught on and changed the entrance to a different side so I couldn't see people coming and going.

I'd also tried to take off my clothes just to cool my body. I peeled off the jogging suit they had given me, stripping down to my shorts. On account of the chains, though, I couldn't get the shirt past my wrists or the pants past my ankles. I also pushed all the blankets and the mat to one end of the closet so that I could lie on the bare floor, which would cool me down a little.

The odor in the closet was horrible, of course. They handled this by opening the door and spraying me with an aerosol can of room deodorizer. Then they'd spray the closet.

During my 564 days as a hostage the number of guards fluctuated. They were a tightly-knit group of zealots who actively advanced the interest of the fanatical Islamic Jihad. The cadre, composed of Abu Ali, Badr, Fadl, Michael, Mahmoud, and Sayeed, were the nucleus of experienced personnel around which other guards were trained.

My first two guards, whose names I didn't know, were kind and considerate. It was difficult to communicate with them because of a language barrier, but I could sense they were not at ease with their employment. It was only a job, temporary at best. One repaired air conditioners and refrigerators but spare parts were hard to come by and he was out of work. When we were moved, after Jerry Levin's escape, I did not see these two again. I missed them. My new guards lacked any sort of human compassion.

Most of my guards were young men between the ages of eighteen and twenty-one. They were victims of a type of

wretched child abuse. Their formal education was ended at an
early age. Instead of books, they were given automatic weapons
and were propagandized to hate and kill. Day in, day out they
played the same cassette over and over again. It was a tape of
fanaticism, a call for the death of all Westerners. (What a relief
it was one day when all the guards left except Fadl, who replaced
the cassette with one of soft classical music. They were not
allowed to listen to music for it was haram, an evil.)

How does one shred the propaganda of hate and death that
is so deeply embedded in a human heart and soul? I saw my
young guards as victims of mind control by their leaders and by
the peer pressure of machismo.

Ironically, as program director of CRS, I knew all too well
that the Shiite community was exploited and oppressed by the
groups in power in Lebanon. They were the poorest of the poor
and their cause was my cause. This radical group of Shiites
would not accept any of CRS' assistance if it came from U.S.
government funds—what they called "Satan's money." They
would, however, accept financial assistance if it was from the
American Catholic Church.

From the beginning I wondered why these people wanted to
keep me imprisoned. I was not their enemy. I had no hate toward
them and could not comprehend their violence toward me. It was
inhuman, stupid. I did not want to get caught up with "the eye
for an eye, tooth for a tooth" mentality. Violence only begets violence. There are intelligent, peaceful ways to resolve conflict. I
believe that the more we actively listen to each other, the more
barriers fall. But for the most part, conversations were only one
way.

The chronicle of those days in isolation was hardly more
than a catalog of absurd and pointless indignities, as if it were an
achievement for my captors to instill pain on those already
wounded. One or another of my guards would react in violent
fury to my most innocuous actions.

In one prison where I was chained to a wall a man filled
with hate approached me. I have no idea why he was there or

who he was. Through my blindfold I saw that he wore a pair of cowboy boots with copper tips. All of a sudden he stood right on my forehead. Embedded into the sole of his shoe were little pieces of stone. He pressed his foot on me like he might squash an insect or a cigarette butt. I said to him, in all of that pain, "Listen, I am not an insect. I am a person of worth, a person of dignity. I'm loved, I'm redeemed, and I do have a destiny."

The guards liked to mock me. They'd put their automatic weapons on my lap and say "Look, look! Look where they're made!" I would tell them, "I don't want to touch any of your instruments of violence." "No, you don't have to touch. Just look! Look!" And they were made either in Israel or the United States. They thought that was pretty funny.

Once they handed me a book saying "Here's a Bible." I kissed it and just held onto it. Later I found out it wasn't a Bible, but a book by Saul Alinski, the community organizer from Chicago.

They'd get mad at me mostly in their paranoia that I had seen them and tell me to stand in the closet with my hands over my head. To do this for any length of time was really painful for me. When the guards weren't around I'd drop my arms, smile, and mumble, "you stupid s.o.b.'s." When I heard them returning, I'd put my hands up again.

One day the guard named Sayeed told me to open my mouth. "What are those silver things in your mouth?" he demanded as he looked in.

"Those are fillings for cavities."

"Those are not fillings. Those are transmitters. You're a CIA spy and we'll give you half an hour to take them out."

What could I do? In the darkness of my closet my anxiety became unbearable, and I prayed in anguish, "Oh God, please don't let them be serious." I was simply terrified that, since I did not take them out, they'd just bash in my face to collect the fillings. The threat was never carried out. It was another one of Sayeed's cruelties, this guard who on different occasions had pounded my ears, hit me until I was black and blue, who had spun me around like a top, and who had kicked me in the stomach.

I kept reminding the guards that I was not CIA. "If anything, I'm VIA—Vatican Intelligence Agency."

The guards were watching television one night in the darkness of their room. I was asleep, wearing the blindfold with pieces of tissue under it and over my eyes, which were infected, hoping to keep them a little cleaner. One of the guards woke me to give me a drink of something and as he did, the tissue fell out. It was dark in there, and they thought my whole blindfold had fallen and I had seen them. They did tremendous violence to me, kicking, beating, and whacking me. Having just come out of a deep sleep, it was all so surreal.

Later they took me to the toilet and noticed how black and blue I was. Sayeed asked, "Where did you get those?" I said "Sayeed, you gave those to me." He never hit me after that, ever. Sometimes he'd do other cruel things. Once, for example, he knelt right on my stomach. He thought it was funny but it was extremely painful.

I snore when I sleep. The guards would open the closet door, wake me, and say, "You're not allowed to snore." I would say, "Snoring is something you cannot control. It's an irrational act." I don't know that they understood that last part. But my snoring caused them sufficient grief that one night they came to me while I was sleeping and sprayed deodorant in my mouth. I still snored.

Occasionally they would take me out of the closet and while blindfolded, spin me like a top. As any child knows, you become dizzy and lose your balance, falling or walking into things. On one of these occasions, in my blind disequilibrium, I walked into a wall, hitting my head with tremendous force. The resulting wound bled. The guards were apparently shocked at this, and apologized. We never played this game again.

One night they took me out of the closet to cut my hair which by that time was quite long. They arranged me so that while my blindfold was off I would be facing the wall, on which I could see the projected shadows of myself, the man cutting my hair, and the other one guarding me. Afterward, they came into the clothes closet and beat me because, they said, I looked at them, which I hadn't done precisely to avoid getting beaten. This was a real learning experience for me—it was dangerous to see a shadow.

With my blindfold on, I could look down the line of my nose and see the floor—more so if I tilted my head back. One morning as I was walking back from my trip to the toilet, I noticed my spoon on the floor. It was in a pile of garbage. I picked it up and cleaned it—licked it really—and put it underneath my sleeping pad. The guards saw this and accused me of concealing the spoon as a weapon to use against them. So they beat me, pounding against my ears with open fists. In addition to the pain, it caused a significant, permanent loss of hearing in my left ear.

Scripture says we are only to bless, not curse anyone. One day the guards gave me a tremendous beating, probably because they accused me of seeing them. Speaking in Latin, I yelled out *"Ab illo benedicaris in cuius honore cremaberis. I nonmine Patris, et Filii, et Spiritus Sancti. Amen."* It's the blessing for incense and translated means, "Be blessed by him in whose honor you shall be burnt. In the name of the Father, and of the Son, and of the Holy Spirit. Amen."

I looked up to the heavens and said to God, "It's a blessing, isn't it?"

In another incident the guards asked me to write about the Society of St. Lazarus. I had never heard of it, but since Jesus raised Lazarus from the dead I thought perhaps the society was one that looked after poor people who were sick. I had no glasses yet, and I tried to write this on a piece of paper. That's all I wrote down, and in very large print so I could read it. A guard threw it back at me and he said, "Wrong!" Well, I didn't know what else to write. I just said, "I'm sorry, but I know nothing else." I would also hear them asking Terry Anderson and William Buckley to list names of Americans, but they weren't getting anywhere with that either.

There was a young guard named Michael. Michael was a very strange person, one of two guards I believed to have mental problems. I nicknamed them "Sicko" and "Psycho." Michael was Sicko and Badr was Psycho. At times Michael was a really generous guy. He'd fan me with a piece of cardboard to cool my body down because it was so hot in my cubicle. Later when they moved me he would put a fan on me, and if someone turned it off he would get back up from his bed and turn it on again.

But Michael also would fill his mouth with water and then spray me with it. One night I was awakened by the sound of someone eating very loudly. I lifted my blindfold to see what this noise was all about. Looking around in the darkness, my eyes suddenly met Michael's. He sprang at me just as suddenly and began kicking me. He did tremendous violence to me and said, in his very broken English, "I used to love you, now I don't."

Later, when I was living with other prisoners, we told Hajj that Michael should not be a guard, that he had personality flaws. One day he'd be kind, another day, vicious. He and Badr disappeared and we were left with Abu Ali, Fadl, Mahmoud, and Sayeed. Basically, for the first six months—my time of isolation—they were violent toward me. For the remaining thirteen months, they no longer physically abused me.

I never felt the urge to do violence to them. Once I dreamt of being rescued by an American SWAT Team. I refused to leave with them. Instead I stayed behind to attend the wounded guards. I'm not sure that if it really happened, I'd have been such a dreamer.

I told these young men the best gift I could give them would be to educate them for a new Lebanon. They could come and live with us in the United States of America and return home after going to school. They loved that invitation and with a loud sigh they'd say, "They will catch us, arrest us, and put us in prison"— dreams and reality.

Now, years later, I'd like to meet these men and ask, "What was accomplished? Are you in school? Are you married? Do you have any children? What about the house you wished to have in order to marry, do you have one?"

When Jesus speaks to our God in his dying moments, "Father, forgive them; for they do not know what they are doing," I wonder which one comes first—requesting forgiveness and making excuses for his tormentors.

As random as the cruelties were during the period of abuse, occasionally I would receive a kindness. Sometimes one of the original guards from my kitchen prison would visit. Sitting beside me in my little chamber, he would take my hand from under the blankets they'd piled on me against the considerable cold. Then he'd open my fingers and place in my palm a piece of candy, some cookies, or some other small item. None of the other guards knew he did this. This is the same guard, I believe, who removed the choking gag from my mouth when I was being transported from one prison to another in a car trunk.

Sometimes they gave me special food on special occasions. Once in my closet prison I could see a guard eating a pizza. I had not been given any food that day. He had one slice left and kept looking in my direction. Suddenly he got up, opened my closet door and said, "Here, you eat this."

One night in early April several guards took me from the closet, up some stairs to a landing and through a doorway into a chill, evening breeze. I was in the open air! They took off my blindfold. We were on the roof.

I was careful not to look around, mindful of their willingness to beat, even kill me if I saw them. Standing at the building's edge, after so long smothering in the extreme heat of the closet, I gazed out over the marvelous city of Beirut. The moon was full. A breeze was coming off the Mediterranean and I was shaking from the chill. The guards thought it was from fear, but strangely, I was not afraid.

Indeed, because they had removed my blindfold, I was absolutely expecting a bullet through my head. At this roof-edge of my prison life, in the white luminance of moon and stars, with the smell and taste of the salt sea-breeze, I knew love reigned invisibly. In the stark electric glare and grinding murmur of this tortured, fratricidal city, I knew this wasn't the world God created. I heard God's love singing to me and in me, modulating all the world's fantastic dissonances.

I gazed on the terrible beauty of creation, that of God and of humankind, believing that I was going to be executed. I waited for my bullet, not thinking what a terrible sinner I was, not thinking I should be sorry for the bad things I did and the good things I failed to do. Rather I thought "Oh, how beautiful this is! How beautiful! Thank you, Lord Jesus! I love you, Lord Jesus! Thank you for everything!"

Then, unexpectedly, one of the guards said, "We know you have not seen a moon in several months. Not even the sky. Because the moon is so beautiful this evening, we wanted you to see a moon."

CHAPTER FIVE

PILGRIMAGES IN TIME AND MIND

Progress is not merely improving the past; it is moving toward the future.

—Kahill Gibran

The religion of Islam is founded on "five pillars":

FAITH there is no God but Allah and Muhammad is his prophet.

PRAYER the five obligatory prayer times of each day: dawn, noon, afternoon, sunset, and night.

FASTING total abstinence from food and liquids from dawn to sunset during the entire lunar month of Ramadan.

PURIFYING ALMSGIVING an annual payment of a determined percent of a Muslim's property given to the poor or others exclusively named in the Muslim scriptures, the Koran (Qur'an).

PILGRIMAGE a journey to the holy city of Mecca once in each Muslim's lifetime, if financially able.

I don't know how well they practiced the other four pillars, but they observed the duty to pray five times a day "religiously." As my captors spoke to Allah I would address my prayer to

51

the same God, Abba, and continue my two great nourishments: recalling God's word to me in Hebrew and Christian covenants, and celebrating eucharist with my ration of Arabic bread.

One might wonder, what does one do from January to July, alone, quiet, shut off from normal human contact? I would create my own prayer forms—my own litany of familiar saints, my own rosaries and mysteries. Squeezing an orange peel, I wrote with its oil on the wall of my cubicle, "Abba, dear Father, I love you much," and "Jesus is Lord." I used my chains as my prayer beads.

In the darkened confines of my solitary cubicle, I would look at the wall and begin to see something, rather someone, looking at me. I was seeing an image in the natural elements of wood and cement. At first I made out eyes on the wall facing my cubicle, eyes full of compassion, as if compassion itself were looking at me. Gradually, over many days, these images became fuller. They became faces. One was the face of Jesus whose eyes of compassion looked at me and spoke to me, saying, "Do not be afraid."

The other image I saw in the motifs of the cement wall was the face of my mother. When last I saw her alive she was on her death-bed. I was a young priest studying at Catholic University in Washington, D.C. when I was suddenly called home. My mom was dying. I arrived at the hospital and immediately went to the post-operative room. Mom had had a tracheotomy and as she struggled to speak to me I said, "Mom, you need to place your finger on this little hole now in order to speak." So I placed her finger on the little hole in her throat and she said to me, "Did you have lunch?" These were the last words she spoke to me. She died shortly after. Now, here in my prison cubicle was her face, her piercing eyes suffused with a mother's care that said, "I'm still looking after you."

It was very strange to me, that in the randomness and uncertainty of my days, after the journeys which began in the belly of a truck and could have ended with my lifeless body being dumped and never found, in each new prison these two images

Pilgrimages in Time and Mind 53

were my constant solace and company.

Being held hostage was a moment-to-moment struggle not to despair. When despair seemed the very air I breathed I had to try not to despair in that despair. Being allowed to go to the toilet only once a day, and having to eat off the floor, gave me a sense of being an animal. I had to keep telling God, "I am not an animal. I'm a person of worth and dignity. I am loved. I am redeemed. And I do have a destiny."

As I sought spiritual nourishments, particularly in my clothes closet, certain hazards attended my solitary prayer life. I had experiences that rarely happen to a person in or out of body. I was afraid they were caused by drugs the guards had given me without my knowing it. Scenes from scripture would invade my mind with peculiar power. I recall especially the conversion of St. Paul en route to Damascus in the Acts of the Apostles. Even more strongly, I had a sense of being out of body, already present to God in my celebration of Easter.

In fact, I became worried that some of my prayer forms were making me go mad. They would run through my head like a tune I couldn't shake. I even stopped praying the "Jesus Prayer" because I was finding it difficult to stay in touch with reality. Despite such difficulty, one source of great succor was the mental pilgrimages I made deep into my past. I went back to who I was historically because, I suppose as a hostage, I felt so ripped out of history. I believe that all hostages go back in memory through their historical being, recalling the details of their existence prior to their captivity. I desperately needed to overcome this incredible impoverishment of being, the result of being forced to exist, as it were, outside of time. I worked hard to see myself again in a historical context. The darkness of night and the darkness of the blindfold helped me to make these pilgrimages and vividly recall the persons, places, sounds, sights, and smells that were Marty Jenco.

Joliet, Illinois, is where I was born and where I spent most of my early life, though our family moved several times around that area. In fact, one of my earliest memories—I must have been about four years old—is of moving. We were moving to our third house and my mom and I were the last of the family to leave. She was sweeping the living room and I was sitting on the stoop of the front porch waiting to go to our new home. Our new house was in a very wooded area and as a child I played frequently in the woods.

My early years always seemed a very special time in my life—growing up in a large Catholic family with three brothers and three sisters, nourished and strengthened by Czech-Slovak traditions and foods, and living in a blue-collar town.

Because of our early moves, I didn't make first communion until third grade. I spent first grade in a Catholic school; second, the year for first communion, in a public school; and third grade in a Catholic school again when we moved to our final home in Joliet. It was on the east side of town in a section called Ridgewood.

Our home was so close to the Catholic church, St. Bernard's, that on Sunday we would have to keep the dogs in the house with the windows closed (even in summer) and make sure the duck didn't quack or the roosters didn't crow during Masses.

Living so close to the Catholic church made it easy to be an altar boy. Sometimes it was too easy. If another altar boy didn't show up, the Franciscan sister in charge of scheduling would call early in the morning asking if I were awake and if I could serve Mass. My sisters, who were already up, would always say, "yes." I would protest to them, "But I wasn't up. You woke me up." Sometimes it annoyed me.

I could be pretty wily, like most kids. But I learned early that crime didn't pay. In my case, living next to the church had almost everything to do with learning that lesson. St. Bernard's was a two-story building, a combination school and church. The school was on the second floor and one classroom overlooked our back-yard. We raised funds to support the school partly through an annual festival. One year during the festival, I walked into the classroom where the pastor, Father Francis, stored the carnival prizes, including a big box of balloons. I grabbed a mittful and threw them out the window knowing that they'd land in our backyard and I could just pick them up.

The next Saturday—the day we regularly went to confession—my mother asked me, "Are you going to go to confession today?" "Mom, I don't want to go to Father Francis. I stole balloons. I would like to go downtown to go to confession," I told her. Bus fare was a nickel down and a nickel back so my mother gave me a dime.

While I was in the bathroom cleaning up, Father Francis came in the back door and said, "Where's Larry?" My mom said, "He's in the bathroom cleaning up to go downtown to go to confession. He stole balloons from you and he doesn't want you to hear his confession." I heard my mother tell him that and I came out of the bathroom and Father Francis said, "If you wanted balloons, all you had to do was ask. You didn't have to steal them." I looked at my mother and said, "You're not getting the dime back, either."

As a child I believed everything and lived partly in a world of make-believe. I believed Santa Claus came down chimneys. Sometimes my parents would find me looking up the chimney and they'd say, "What are you doing there?" I would say, "Maybe Santa Claus dropped something. I was just checking it out."

I believed in little people who lived in little houses and I would make tents by putting blankets over chairs and then pretend to live in them. The strange thing is, as a hostage I remember being very cold and it was as if I were back in my little tents, fantasizing about playing in a cold, dreary place, trying to survive in that.

As a child, I thought the tabernacle on the altar in church was literally the house of Jesus. I wanted to see inside, to see his table and chairs and his bedroom. I knew the only time I'd ever get the chance to see that was on Good Friday of Holy Week when the altar was stripped and the tabernacle opened. I wanted to serve Mass on Good Friday so I could look in to see what his house looked like. When I finally had a chance to look in, I was shocked to discover nothing was inside.

I also believed in the Easter Bunny. It was part of how we celebrated Easter in our home. Both my parents were big on Easter baskets and Easter eggs. We would color the eggs Holy Saturday evening, and then on Easter we'd awaken to find a basket under our bed. One morning, however, I woke up and caught my sister Mae putting the basket under my bed. "You're the Easter Bunny!" I said. She put her finger to her lips, "Shhhh!"

I got both hand-me-downs and hand-me-ups because both my older and my younger brothers were bigger than I. But at Easter time I would get a new suit. I remember one Holy Saturday visiting my Grandma Jenco wearing my new Easter clothes and bringing her an Easter gift.

My dad was Slovak-American, and my mother was Bohemian-American. My dad worked a 4-11 p.m. shift at the Texaco Company in Lockport, Illinois. On most days when we came home from school, he was still there, just about to leave for work. If we got home before he left, my dad expected a hug and kiss from us. And if we didn't greet him that way he would say, "Am I not good enough for a hug and a kiss?" To this day I can remember the smell of my father's aftershave lotion.

In these pilgrimages across time I sought out and reconnected with moments when I was very much present to my family—special occasions such as Christmas or Easter, birthday celebrations or baptisms, confirmations or first communions. These were the important events in my young life. We were a close family and seeing aunts, uncles, and grandparents at these times was always so special.

My family tells a story about me as a child making my first communion. I was sitting at the table next to my father and I said, "My teacher says we receive Jesus at communion, but it's round. Jesus is round. I need to know which way does Jesus go down? Does he go head first or feet first?" They tell me that my father had this look of utter shock and I'm not sure if I ever got an answer from him. After that, every time our family had a first communion, even of a cousin or a grandchild, they would remember that story and ask, "Which way does Jesus go down?"

My maternal grandmother was Mary Voda Cirhan, a well-educated Bohemian-American who lived in Chicago and moved to a farm in Minnesota. I remember from childhood visits that she suffered terrible headaches. Whenever they happened she would tie a cloth around her head. I have a mental picture of her sitting on a lawn chair with this cloth wrapped tightly around her head.

In captivity I ripped a piece of blue cloth from my blanket, and whenever I got a headache, I would wrap it tightly around my head and the pain would stop. Later when I talked to doctors about this, they dismissed it, saying, "Oh, that's psychosomatic," or something or other.

I left Joliet as an adolescent to enter the Carmelites order in Niagara Falls, New York. From there I returned to Illinois to join the Servites, who eventually sent me to Riverside, California, to study philosophy. En route through Denver I saw a mountain for the first time. It totally overwhelmed me. Then in California I saw an ocean for the first time. To this day I feel overwhelmed in the presence of either, and sometimes greatly depressed. Perhaps because of their immensity.

I also studied in Rome and was ordained there in 1959. I went home to celebrate my first Mass in my parish in Joliet. For two years after ordination I taught at our Servite minor seminary in Elgin, Illinois. In 1962, I was sent to Denver, Colorado, as associate pastor of Our Lady of Mount Carmel parish and as a full-time teacher of religion in the parish primary and secondary schools.

In my mental pilgrimages, I also returned to the places I worked as my career developed—North Yemen, India, Thailand, and Australia.

Initially I went to India to work with Servites in a new foundation in Mahabalipuram but ended up working as an administrator in a hospital for differently-abled children. I had gone to India with a global vision: I was going to change the world. But the poverty was so overwhelming, so provoking of despair, that it completely challenged my understanding of myself in relation to the world, and forced me to refocus my vision and sense of purpose.

A child helped teach me that. On my way to Mahabali-puram, I met this child, a polio victim unable to walk, begging in the dust. Through my interpreter I asked the lad if he might like to come to Mithra Hospital where I worked in Madras. The young lad said that he would have to get his parents' permission. We then met his parents, got their approval, and brought him to the hospital.

Around that time I became seriously ill with hepatitis and was scheduled to leave India for treatment. Before leaving, the staff and patients had a farewell party for me. As a gift to me this young boy walked to me with the help of crutches and calipers. I understood then the need to refocus my vision, to help one child at a time, one person at a time.

In the prison quiet of my clothes closet or cubicles, I would break spontaneously into song. I couldn't recall any of the most popular religious songs. Instead, I found myself singing hymns I learned as a child, "Oh Mary, we crown thee with blossoms today, Queen of the Angels, Queen of the May," or, "On this day, O beautiful mother." Mary's crowning as Queen of the May was something we did both in church and at home. I remembered creating our own May altars in the backyard—a remembrance suffused with fragrance of lilacs and peonies.

Whenever my family planned a picnic or some sort of outing, my mother would put the statue of the Blessed Mother out in the backyard so that we would have nice weather. But she would always get up early in the morning to make sure that it was a nice day. If it was raining, she would bring the statue back in, hoping, I suspect, that we wouldn't lose faith. A story told in my family recounts my mother once finding the statue in a bucket of water. Apparently my brother Joe was angry with Mary because the weather was bad and we weren't going to go on a picnic, and he dumped the statue in a bucket.

We had a pet duck that some of us had grown very fond of. Its quacking eventually brought about its demise, though, as it tended to reach a peak of exuberance during the pastor's sermons. Finally, the pastor asked my parents if we would kill it. My dad killed the duck and we served it for a Sunday meal, to which, of course, we invited our pastor. None of us ate any of it. We were not too pleased with him.

We also had a rooster that even our dog was afraid of. More so my younger sister, Sue. One day in one of my prison pilgrimages, I remembered a scene of the rooster chasing her. Whenever we wanted to keep her in the house, we would tell her, "The rooster's outside," and she'd remain indoors. I sometimes wondered how she survived us.

On Sunday night we would listen to the Catholic Hour, sometimes also to the Slovak Hour, even though we didn't understand Slovak. My dad was a sentimental man to whom tears came easily. I realized this not long after we got our first television. Whenever something sad was on, my dad wouldn't hesitate to cry.

In mid-June between my junior and senior years at the Servite high school seminary, my dad and mom drove up to Elgin, Illinois, to bring me home for summer vacation. My dad had bought my mother a new car for her birthday so they could visit relatives and see me on "visiting Sunday." My mom's birthday was June 28, and the next day my brother Dick, who had been drafted, was leaving. My family decided to celebrate both occasions at once with a family cookout in our backyard and invited friends and relatives.

On the morning of June 29, we all went down to the train station to say goodbye to Dick. My dad said to my mother, "I just don't feel well," and my mom suggested he visit the doctor since we were already downtown. He did and the doctor put my dad in the hospital. My mom came home from the hospital that evening and asked me to go see my dad. I said, "Mom, he just went into the hospital. It would probably be better if we didn't annoy him with a visit but allowed him to get some rest." But she said, "Oh, no, please go. You don't see him much when you're at school. Go see him." So I went up to visit my dad.

When I arrived he was resting. His sister Sue also had come to visit and we both sat outside and somewhat away from his room in a visitor's lounge. At one point I looked up and noticed several nursing sisters running into my father's room. I walked in and saw Father Francis, who had just anointed my dad, giving him the Blessed Sacrament. He then placed a brown scapular around my dad's neck, and prayed with him. My dad said to me simply, "I think my goose is cooked." A sister, cradling dad in her arms, began praying the Litany of the Saints. She must have known my dad was dying. But I didn't know. I was just a teenager and had never known my dad to be ill for even a day in his life, much less seen anyone die. I heard my father's voice responding to the litany: "Pray for us . . . pray for us . . . pray for us . . ." and then silence. He died, leaving us with those words: "Pray for us."

Sometimes on these pilgrimages, I cried as I remembered people, places, and things. Sometimes I found myself laughing over an event that struck me funny. One such event occurred when I was ordained.

My mother couldn't come to Rome for my ordination because of poor health but my two aunts made the trip. Getting the first blessing of a newly-ordained priest in the family was very important. My two aunts jostled to get in position to receive the first blessing. I chuckled because I really gave my first blessing to my mom and dad—long distance—my dad who was present to God and my mom who was living in Joliet. But as my two aunts struggled to get into position to receive my first blessing, someone took a photograph, and I have this marvelous smile because the older of the two, Aunt Ann, outmaneuvered Aunt Sue.

During these months of isolation, on my historical pilgrimage back to our gentle God and to people who had touched my life, I found I had marvelous remembrances. Some were very encouraging; some very sustaining and affirming; and others were remembrances of pain, suffering, and loss.

I remember sitting at table with a group of brother Servites, one of whom was ultra-conservative. He was really needling me.

At one point in the conversation another Servite said to me, "You should listen to your brother Servite. He has a Master's in Theology from a university in the Midwest." I looked up from my plate and I said, "I would question the university that gave him a degree." I looked into his eyes when I said that and saw the tremendous hurt. I was so sorry. As a hostage, with memory a vivid, constant companion, I once again saw the eyes, the hurt I caused and said, "I am sorry I caused you such pain, such hurt. I had no right to say that."

Perhaps it may seem a luxury to do a historical scan of one's life for days on end, to make an effort, to say, "Where was I yesterday? What city was I in? How old was I?" and then to continue on a pilgrimage in mind. Is it a regression, or a re-membering of what only seems lost? A conscious act of bringing into present time those persons, places, sounds, sights, and smells in which we discover that nothing, in truth, is ever really lost?

I derived much comfort and consolation from the process. Although the months of isolation were often tedious, I had the luxury of reflecting on my life. Meeting people I loved greatly and asking their forgiveness was a catharsis for me. It brought me laughter and sadness as well as a kind of escape from my physical surroundings.

CHAPTER SIX

TRUST IN THE LORD

Hear, O Lord, when I cry aloud,
be gracious to me and answer me!
"Come," my heart says, "seek his face!"
Your face, Lord, do I seek.

—Psalm 27:7-8

In April, sometime before Easter 1985, I was chained to a wall in an apartment bedroom. The guards were sitting on a bed opposite my wall, watching television one night. The program was in Arabic, but I understood some of it. I think it was called "Good Friday in Jerusalem." The guards asked one of the other prisoners to explain what Good Friday and Easter were all about. The man gave a marvelous explanation of these holiest days in the Christian calendar. I didn't know who he was at the time, though I believed him to be the same man I'd seen chained to the bed.

This was all quite curious to me, because I had already celebrated Easter not long before while living in the clothes closet. By counting the knots I'd tied in a string, one for each day, I had figured the date for Ash Wednesday. To observe the first day of the Lenten season, I took some dirt from the bathroom floor, blessed it, and signed my forehead with it, saying, "Remember, Marty Jenco, that you are dust, and unto dust you shall return."

By continuing my knotted-string calendar I counted down to what I thought was Easter and celebrated eucharist in my closet. I suppose there was some poignancy in spending Holy Week as a hostage in chains, celebrating it a week early. Now I learned

I had been mistaken in my calculations. Yet I knew there was only one thing to do about it: celebrate it again!

And so I did. Not that it was easy before, but this time it was a little more difficult. Chained to a wall in the guards' presence, I had to rise very early to avoid their surveillance, celebrating eucharist for my second Easter in pre-dawn darkness.

I always retained a piece of the eucharistic Christ, clinging to the Lord especially in moments of violence, sadness, boredom, or fear. One day I was holding Christ's body in a closed hand and one of the guards noticed and asked, "What do you have in your hand?" Opening my clenched fist, I showed him the small piece of bread and said, "This is Jesus." He stood in uncomprehending silence.

In one of my prisons they built cubicles for us. Mine was in one corner of the room, Terry Anderson's in another, and William Buckley's in the center of the room.

During this time we all got very ill, particularly Mr. Buckley. I think he had pneumonia because he was coughing and dehydrating. He repeatedly asked the guards for tea, water, or other liquids. I had a bad cold, perhaps even a fever. The guards refused us any water, and I said to one, "Sayeed, we need water." He said, "No, my mother said you should not drink water when you have a cold or a fever." I said, "Sayeed, I think it's the exact opposite. Listen, I will do it for one day but tomorrow, please, give me some water."

I couldn't help asking the "why" questions—"why me?" "why this?" One morning I heard Mr. Buckley groan, "Why, God? I've been through so much. Why this?" And then I recalled the groaning "why" question Jesus asked during his dying moments, "My God, my God, why have you abandoned me?"

Oh, yes, at times I complained to God. Then the awareness began to set in that, for all the passion I might wring from my heart to fuel this petition, "why" questions are simply not going to be answered.

I'd tell God, "I'm not Job, I want to go home now." Or, "Listen, God, I cannot make promises to you. I cannot bargain with you. I came in as Marty Jenco, I want to leave as Marty Jenco. I want to be accepted in my sinfulness and in my holiness."

I do not believe the adage "the clothes make the man," but I wanted quite desperately to be able to leave dressed in what I wore when I was kidnapped. From prison to prison I carried my gray pants and sweater and my white shirt so I could go out wearing the clothes I had on when captured. Pieces of my clothes had been taken before and when that happened I would be devastated. It was so important to me to hold fast to these things. Shortly before Mr. Buckley died, the guards took my white shirt, gray sweater, and pants. I think they buried Mr. Buckley in them.

Then I experienced a transforming moment. I had been saving a little button that had come off my coat the morning I was kidnapped. It was very important to me and I would take it from prison to prison. If I misplaced it I would search for my button. One day in all this madness I said to God, "Oh, you can have the button," and I threw it away. "Cling to nothing material" became my motto. "Rely on and trust in the Lord."

One evening, the guards brought in a television with a VCR. They wanted me and one other hostage to see a video on the gestures of Muslims at prayer. I was to look only at the television and not around the room or at anyone who was with me. I didn't know it, but Ben Weir was the other hostage watching with me.

Sitting next to me was an interpreter who spoke English quite well. He explained the video, but he had a particularly vicious case of halitosis. Every time he spoke to me he breathed in my face and, hungry and depleted and otherwise generally miserable, I very nearly vomited. And I kept thinking, "Oh, I absolutely mustn't do that. They'll just think I'm disgusted by their religion and be terribly offended." I bit my fingers hard, barely controlling what was nearly uncontrollable.

In my mind I still have those impressions of Muslims at prayer, up and down and bowing, such that when I see Muslims at prayer now, I flashback painfully into that time and place.

Around this time—probably in May—some very strange things began to occur. Our lives were suddenly turned upside down. The guards had completely reversed our living patterns, as if days were nights and nights were days. My anxiety level went soaring with the pigeons as I wondered why they slept all day and stayed up all night. Why did they give me food only during the night, not in the day? Why did they allow me to go to the toilet only during the night, not during the day? I really wondered if I was in the process of madness.

It was Ramadan, the month-long period of fasting kept as one of the "pillars" of Islam. Fasting means total abstinence from food and liquids from dawn to sunset. In addition, married Muslims must also refrain from sexual intercourse from dawn to sunset. They may, however, enjoy all these things during the night. But I didn't put that together. All I knew was that the inverted pattern of my days heightened my anxiety.

My glasses were a source of great anxiety for me. I had left them behind when we were moved out of my kitchen prison in the Bekaa mountains back in February.

While chained and blindfolded in the cubicle, Hajj would walk into my cubicle and simply touch me, silently and gently. I don't know why he did this. One day in June, I suspect it was Hajj who walked into my cubicle, touched me, and put something near my hand. I picked it up and—my glasses! I was so pleased to get my glasses back.

I think I got them back because the guards had given me a Bible to read. Of course I couldn't see the print without my glasses. They would accuse me of not being a good man because I didn't read the Bible and I'd say, "I can't read without my glasses."

No sooner had I gotten them back from Hajj, than one of the guards took them from me again and removed the screws from the ear pieces. And they wouldn't stay on without the arms. I was quite distraught over this and asked a guard named Fadl why the other guard would remove the earpiece screws. All Fadl said was that it was crazy, that the other guard was crazy.

I thought of putting string through the hinges in place of

the confiscated screws, so that I wouldn't constantly have to hold the frames. But I couldn't see the tiny holes.

During this time I was actually chained to another person: the chain attached to my ankle was threaded through a hole in the base of the wall between my cubicle and another room and attached to someone in that adjacent room. So whenever he jerked I would feel it. It was one of those annoying things in life. You keep having your leg jerked. Under these conditions, sleep was never restful.

William Buckley was very, very sick, dying in fact. This was when the guards moved me out of my cubicle and chained me to a wall in the corridor, a wall that faced both the kitchen and the toilet. There I could observe the traffic in the hallway in spite of my blindfold. I saw the guards carrying an obviously delirious William Buckley to the toilet. He would sit on the floor but think he was on the toilet. I heard him say, "I would like some poached eggs on toast please." All this madness going on there! They lifted him up off the floor and brought him back to his room.

A few nights later, there was a lot of commotion. I could look through my blindfold and see a man being carried out. I asked Sayeed, "How is my American brother doing?" and he said, "He's not doing too well." I asked him, "Where are you taking him?" Sayeed said, "He's very, very sick. He needs to have some good air and some sunlight so we're bringing him to another prison where he'll get well again." Two days later I asked Sayeed again, "How is my brother doing?" and he said, "He died." I could sense that he was grieved. I think Sayeed and Mr. Buckley had become good friends because I would hear their frequent conversations. Mr. Buckley once said to Sayeed, "Sayeed, you owe me one."

Sayeed should not have told me that Mr. Buckley died because later he came back and told me, "I was just kidding you. Mr. Buckley didn't die." In support of this deception he said, "You can see how many people pass by here barefoot to go to the toilet in the morning. Just count the feet and you will see that he is well now." The number of feet were the same, but it was actually David

Jacobson who was now passing by. But I did not know that. Jacobson had been kidnapped recently and in fact had been put in my cubicle when they moved me to the corridor.

Because of Mr. Buckley's death, they kidnapped a Lebanese Jewish doctor to look after us and the other hostages. That evening he came to the corridor where I was chained to check my health.

It was now late June and I hadn't washed since I was taken from my kitchen prison on February 14. I had developed a terrible infection in my eyes, which continually secreted a liquid that would cake up and become very annoying. My blindfold was a filthy cotton t-shirt and I placed folded toilet paper between my eyes and the cloth.

When the doctor came to me, after he checked my heart and blood pressure, I asked if he would take a look at my eyes. He took off the blindfold, examined my eyes and told the guards who were making the rounds with him that I had an eye infection. He threw away the blindfold and said, "This man cannot wear this blindfold anymore. He needs to rinse his eyes with tea," and he prescribed Terramycin for the infection.

The young guards were very faithful in putting the Terramycin in my eyes—which was very strange because I would have to look at them while they did. The guards never allowed me to rinse my eyes as the doctor had said. But I decided not to try to live without the blindfold. I knew the rule was they warned us under threat of death not to see them. It was just too painful to try to keep my eyes closed every time I heard a noise or a door open. So I searched in the garbage around my bed, found my blindfold, and put it back on.

One curious physical symptom was a burning sensation in my extremities—hands, head, and feet. Perhaps it was due to my high blood pressure. In any case, it was extremely painful.

The doctor also prescribed Dyazide for my blood pressure. Initially, the guards were very good about supplying me with the Dyazide. But later they wouldn't give it to me at times. Perhaps they were out of it, probably because they didn't have the money to buy it. So I learned to salvage some by reducing my dosage. I'd squirrel away what was left for those days when they didn't give me any. It was a very important medication for me, as my condition was apparently serious.

One day they forgot to close the window in the toilet so there in the corridor I stood up on my mat and looked out. I could see a tree. A eucalyptus! I wept. Because of the guards' threats to kill me if I ever saw them, I was very sight-conscious and didn't want to be caught looking. But I did pray, "God, you can have any one of my five senses, but I would like to keep my sight." How I missed being able to see God's creation!

I would salvage tissue paper from the toilet as hankies because they wouldn't give us any tissue. I would hang the used tissues around my mat to dry so I could reuse them—three or four times before throwing them away. Since my release, I use a piece of tissue once and throw it away, and sometimes before it even lands I'm amazed at myself, remembering how I used to hoard and reuse them.

Finally they gave me a water bottle and a urine bottle. The urine bottle was the same size as the water bottle. But most of the things we ate had water in them, which meant that the urine bottle would be full and I'd need to urinate again long before I'd get to empty it. It just didn't work well. I would ask the guards to empty my urine bottle, and they would get very angry. I would say to them, "If it's offensive to you, I will empty it myself." Grudgingly, they gave in and emptied it. I was always anxious about their emptying my urine bottle, especially toward evening, since I would wake up in the middle of the night needing to urinate. At times it was painful.

On my morning trips to the toilet, there would only be one towel there. Always the same towel, almost always wet. All five Americans imprisoned there used that towel to wipe their hands and face. It was never cleaned once. Later I would share with my brother hostages in other prisons about that towel: how we all tried to wring it out, reuse it and reuse it.

Then one day Sayeed said, "You may take a bath." So they

filled the tub with water. One at a time, we took a bath—Ben Weir, David Jacobson, Tom Sutherland, Marty Jenco, Terry Anderson—all in the same water.

Sayeed would say to me, "You must do some exercise." Do some exercise?! There I was standing, blindfolded, wearing my shorts, maybe a t-shirt, and he would say "Do push-ups." And I would think: Wait a minute, I've been chained to walls or cramped in a closet since January. Do push-ups?! I told him, "I cannot do push-ups." He got very angry at that and said, "We want you to run in place." Well, all right I thought. I'll try to run in place. "Try" was as far as I could get. It was so perfectly stupid, so completely inane—and I said, "This is stupid. There's no way I'm going to run in place. It's extremely painful. I will not do this." Of course, they again became very angry with me—an emotion they must have enjoyed, considering how easily they were provoked. So I guess I was doing them a favor.

CHAPTER SEVEN

SWEET TOGETHERNESS

*Christ breaks the power of reigning sin and sets the
prisoner free.*

—*Charles Wesley*

There were periods in captivity when I obsessed about food—dreaming of food while sleeping, and thinking of food for hours when awake. One food that always came to mind was pickled herring. I don't know why, but I was always dreaming about eating pickled herring. Sometimes I would find myself chomping on things when there was nothing there. I saved orange peelings and would munch on them on days when the guards gave me no food.

The routine of my diet I suppose caused this obsessing. For breakfast I was usually given tea, wedges of cream cheese, and pita bread. Today I see that brand of cheese with the trademark cow on the wrapper and I'm taken back to my hostage life. Occasionally the guards would give us extra wedges. I'd try to salvage things like onions from other meals to make it taste a little better.

Lunch was rice or fava beans and bread. The portions were pretty generous. I wanted to remember the names on the bread bags, knowing it might indicate where we were being held. Then I could try to find the bakery after my release. Sometimes they would provide some fresh vegetables or some olives. The evening meal usually consisted of Arabic bread and some kind of sugar compote with seeds.

One evening the guards were eating chicken with lemon—at

least that's what it smelled like. But because I had fallen asleep and started to snore, they took a lemon they had sliced open and threw it at me full force. The juices went into my eyes. My eyes were infected then and the stinging was so painful.

I told them I had an upset stomach and needed some medication for it. Instead they said, "Eat a lemon," and gave me one. I was surprised that it helped, then I used an upset stomach as a pretext to ask for a lemon. I'd lie to them, saying I had an upset stomach, and they would give me a lemon. I'd save it and use it on the food to make it taste a little better. With a little salt it was very good, and if I did have an upset stomach it usually made me feel better.

The building where I was held first in a clothes closet, then in a cubicle, and afterward chained to a wall in the hallway was very close to the Beirut airport. When planes landed or took off, the building would shake, and the smell of airplane exhaust would invade the room.

There was much fighting around the building. One night the guards brought us flak jackets to protect us against stray shrapnel or bullets. They were very heavy—lined with lead or some other heavy metal—and covered us from neck to knees. I told the guards, "I don't want to wear it. It's too hot and I can't stand it." When I tried to take it off and slip it down the chains, the guards would force me to put it on again. I said, "No, I don't want to wear this. It's just too hot. I can't breath."

Mr. Buckley said I was foolish for not wanting to wear the flak jacket, but I thought, "My head doesn't have a flak jacket on it. Or a bomb could come through the wall and smash me to smithereens." But the guards insisted I wear it, so when I saw through the shower curtain that they were coming to check me out, I would quickly put it on. For the most part, though, I tried not to wear it.

After Mr. Buckley died, they took us outdoors one night. We were not really blindfolded, but we had to keep our heads down and walk quietly. I didn't really keep my head down and looked around. The night was moonlit and the stars were out. It was about the first of July and we were being moved to our next prison.

This would be my fifth prison. In a six month period they had taken me from the kitchen prison, where I spent nearly a month, to a location higher in the Baalbek mountains after Jerry Levin escaped. I was there from February 14 to March 15 and then taken to an apartment in the southern suburbs of Beirut where I was kept in a clothes closet until late April. However the owner wanted his apartment back, so we were moved to another apartment in the same building where I was kept first in a cubicle, then chained to a wall in the corridor.

Now we were taken to a one-story school building in the same suburbs where an apartment was located on the roof. The windows were sealed with concrete blocks. The guards took us into a room in the apartment and they told us we could lift our blindfolds when they locked the door. They also warned us that whenever they returned and put the key in the lock before entering, we were to put our blindfolds back on.

Once the door was locked, I asked, "May we speak to one another?" They said, "No, you may not speak to one another." This room was lit by a small blue light and I was chained to one of the walls. I lifted my blindfold and I looked across the room and saw another man also chained to a wall. This was the first time I was in a cell with another person and knew who he was— seeing him fully and speaking with him. He lifted his blindfold and we just looked at each other for a while.

Then he said, "I am Ben Weir." I thought they had killed him. It was just a joy to know he wasn't dead. Our luck was so phenomenal. Even to this day I give praise and thanks to a gentle God for the marvelous gift of seeing Ben in that room with me.

Then he whispered, "I think this room is bugged."

"What makes you think so?" I asked. He pointed to something against the wall, a small container of some sort. I stretched my chain and took hold of it. After my expert examination, I gave him my report, "If it is a bug, it's very cleverly disguised as

A few days before his kidnapping, Father Jenco (right) met with a Maronite priest in the Lebanese mountains while setting up a Catholic Relief Services project there.

Khaled, the man who was driving Father Jenco's car at the time of the kidnapping.

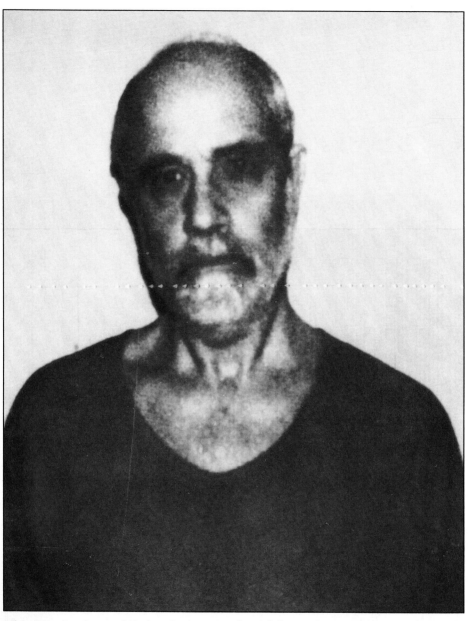

This AP wirephoto of Father Jenco was released during his captivity.

Within hours of his release, news photographs showed Father Jenco with the Syrian Foreign Minister, Farouk Al Sharaa.

Father Jenco with his family who all worked so hard for his release are pictured in a U.S. military plane in Wiesbaden, Germany. Left to right are: Brothers John and Joe, sister Sue Franceschini, Father Jenco, sisters Mae Mihelich and Betty Blair, and brother Richard.

Archbishop of Canterbury Robert Runcie greets Father Jenco.

Reunion with fellow prisoner, Presbyterian minister Rev. Ben Weir, in London.

Father Jenco, his sister Mae Mihelich, and Terry Waite (in the background) meet Pope John Paul II a few days after his release.

Father Jenco is received in the White House by President and Mrs. Reagan.

Huge crowds turn out for Father Jenco's return to Joliet.

Rev. Jesse Jackson, who had worked tirelessly for the release of the hostages, speaks at a welcome home reception in Joliet. Father Jenco tugs on the sleeve of his brother, Richard.

After all the American hostages were released, they gathered in Washington for a reception in their honor. Left to right are Father Jenco, Robert Pohil, Thomas Sutherland, Rev. Ben Weir, Terry Anderson, Alan Steen, Jesse Turner and Joseph Cicippio.

Father Jenco meets with Peg Say, Terry Anderson's sister, former hostages Jerry Levin (left), and Rev. Ben Weir (right), as part of their ongoing efforts to publicize the plight of hostages still in Lebanon.

Friends and cellmates Martin Jenco and Terry Anderson after Anderson's release in 1991.

a room deodorizer." We both burst into laughter.

The room had no windows, but two fans sat in the upper corners of one wall circulating our stale air. That was it.

Ben had the scriptures and a pair of glasses that I could use. Once again my glasses had become a source of anxiety. I had left them behind in my last prison. In time Hajj would bring them to me, with the screws in the earpieces. Then tragically, in the confusion of the guards coming into our room one day, I accidentally sat on them and broke them.

I asked Hajj if he would get me a new pair. He took the broken pair from me and a few weeks later returned with some of the guards. He asked that I extend my hand, palm upwards. He set a pair of glasses in the palm of my hand. My smile must have extended from one ear to the other. Hajj said, "Be careful. These cost three hundred Lebanese pounds." The tone of his voice was not harsh. I could almost hear his smile. I suspect now that he wanted me to go out wearing glasses when I was released.

But during the periods I was without my glasses Ben would share his with me.

Daily, Ben and I worshipped at the Church of the Locked Door. We were sustained by God's word. I would celebrate eucharist one day and Ben would celebrate a communion service the next usually based on 1 Corinthians 11:17-27. Our great nourishments were God's word, God's table, and each other.

Ben wrote out the Nicene Creed in a little booklet they gave us. He also wrote out, from memory, several Presbyterian hymns to sing. These would comprise our hymnal later when the other Americans joined us. They were part of our sustenance and certain words and phrases had special meanings.

Ben was a Presbyterian minister who had come to Lebanon years earlier. He and his wife Carol and their three daughters and son were very much a part of the country. Ben and Carol had intended to remain in Lebanon.

Ben had also once worked in the Oakland-Berkeley area and I had been assigned in Berkeley for three years as prior of the

Servite house of formation at the Graduate Theological Union. So sharing our histories included sharing our experiences of Berkeley—familiar places and people we both knew.

We also both remembered Michael, Sicko of the sado-masochistic comedy team "Psycho and Sicko." At times Michael could be kind. When the other guards turned off the fan they used to cool me off, he would turn it back on. If there was an electrical outage, Michael would fan me with a piece of card-board. Once while doing this he had said, "You hot, you dead." When Michael left the room, Ben and I lifted our blindfolds and he looked at me and said, "You hot, you dead." We burst into laughter. It became a key phrase for us that would provoke a tick-le of relief or even outright laughter when abuse and boredom threatened to merge into idiot bliss.

Ben wore goggles with black tape over the glass as his blind-fold. He would wear nothing else as a blindfold. Whenever the key went into the door, announcing an imminent entry, it was always interesting to watch Ben scrambling around his mat for his goggles.

He was in pretty good shape when I came upon him in that prison. He would do exercises regularly including running in place with his chains banging against the floor.

One day in mid-July the door opened. I was sitting against the wall and through the blindfold could see the guards drag in another hostage. He was barefoot, wearing only shorts and a t-shirt.

He was Tom Sutherland, the Dean of the School of Agriculture at the American University of Beirut. Tom had been kidnapped on June 9, 1985, upon his return from a trip to the U.S. and while en route from the airport to his apartment at the University. Since he was the most recently-captured hostage, he brought us up-to-date—or within a month of up-to-date—on some of the world events we had missed.

As the guards brought him in, they threw a mat on the floor next to mine and sat him down on it. He asked, "Where's my bed?" I thought, "Hmmm. He wants a bed! A little bit unreal, wanting a bed in this place." They started to chain him and he said, "What are those?"

"Chains," they replied.

He said, "Well, I don't want to wear them." And I thought, "Hmmm. He doesn't want to wear them!" I couldn't wait until the guards left so I could lift my blindfold and see what this man was all about.

Later, he explained he had been held captive in what they called "the stalls," a place of death. Our captors had kidnapped some of their own people and executed them there. Tom had a bed in the stalls, but it didn't exactly fit the space he'd been crammed into. He had to fold his mattress partly so that it was more like a chair. But he could sleep on it. He had asked for his "bed" out of that craving for the familiar, the desire of hostages to maintain some fragment of control to help stay the insanity of a captive existence. Nor had he been chained in his last prison either.

We knew we had neighbors in the room next to us. My chain was threaded through a hole in the bottom of a wall and shackled to someone in the next room. I tried to look through but couldn't see anything. The guards must have seen me because they got mad and accused me of the criminal act of attempting to see who our neighbors were, so they moved the chain, passing it instead through the corridor wall. This made it seem very strange then, when one of the guards came in and asked Tom if he'd like to meet a friend and colleague being held in the next room. It was David Jacobson, Director of the American University Hospital.

After that our captors allowed Ben and I and our neighbors to come together to visit and to pray together. They would take Ben, Tom, and me into the next room where we'd hang out with our neighbors Terry Anderson and David Jacobson. We would pray and be nourished by God's word, God's table, and each other. Sometimes Ben led the prayer service. Sometimes I celebrated eucharist.

When I first came into their room, Terry told Hajj that he

was a Catholic and wished to go to confession to me. Hajj responded, "It is not necessary to confess to man. You only need to confess to God." Terry was very obstinate and said, "No, that is not my tradition." Terry was a recovering Catholic coming back into his own faith commitment and the only other Catholic in the group.

Hajj finally honored Terry's request, even pulling everyone else out of the room so that Terry and I had privacy. We stood facing each other and lifted our blindfolds. What a marvelous sight to look into his eyes! I gave praise to God again for the marvelous gift of sight. I realized that I had seen him before. He was the man chained to the bed, whom I had watched through the crack of the door in my closet prison. He was the man who had given that marvelous explanation of Good Friday and Easter to the guards. I listened to this man speak the words, "Bless me Father, for I have sinned." It was an extremely emotional encounter with God, truly a home-coming.

Around this time, our captors made a brilliant discovery. They unearthed an extraordinary secret that had evaded the inner circles of the foremost intelligence communities in the world, not to mention regular government offices, the media, and the average citizen.

To wit: Terry Anderson, David Jacobsen, and Tom Sutherland were spies. I'm sure that not even America's National Security Agency was aware of this. Hajj, whom I saw about once a month, wanted to move them to the stalls, but I argued that they were not spies and he got very angry with me.

They did move Terry, David, and Tom to what the guards said was another prison. But when they opened the door of our room to let in some fresh air, I watched them and I saw them carrying bowls of food down the stairs. I told Ben, "Terry, David, and Tom are not in another prison. They're downstairs somewhere."

Another roommate of Terry and David's before they were moved was Wajd Domani, a Syrian-born Lebanese who was captured in the southern suburbs of Beirut. Apparently his captors thought they had gotten their hands on a Kuwaiti diplomat, but instead what we all got was a pain in the neck.

Wajd, it turned out, was claustrophobic—certainly not his fault—but being held in close quarters with Terry and David and having a cloth blindfold over his head was making him go mad. Because of David's efforts, and with some help from Terry, they calmed him down.

After moving Terry and David, the guards moved Wajd in with us. I was chained to one wall and Ben to the opposite wall. Wajd was in the middle of the room. He rolled over and asked me how long I'd been there and I told him I was kidnapped on January 8. He looked totally shocked, rolled over and asked Ben the same question. Ben replied, "I was kidnapped on May 8, 1984." Wajd actually paled by several degrees, and let a tremendous groan rise from him. We couldn't do much, except encourage him not to give up hope. Wajd was released soon after that. Our captors accepted that, contrary to their fondest hopes, poor Wajd was not a Kuwaiti diplomat, just a Lebanese citizen like themselves.

CHAPTER EIGHT

LEARNING TO FORGIVE

Father, forgive them; for they do not know what they are doing.

—Luke 23:34

On the evening of August 14, our captors told us we were going to be moved to another prison. They instructed us to gather our clothing, our water and urine bottles, and whatever little possessions we had accumulated over the months.

As a hostage, you get very comfortable in your prison, even secure, though the conditions may be horrendous. But as soon as moving is mentioned you become very anxious. Your body reacts, and you experience a great need to go to the toilet almost instantly.

So it was with Ben on this occasion. I remember him saying, "I need to go to the toilet." The guards said, "You can't." But he became more insistent. So after they pushed me out of the room and started me down the stairs, they let Ben go to the toilet.

We didn't leave the building. Our next prison was actually in the basement of the school building. I arrived at the cell alone and looked down the line of my nose and beneath my blindfold to see three additional pairs of feet. They belonged to none other than Terry Anderson, Tom Sutherland, and David Jacobson. Ben Weir joined us shortly. Sweet togetherness! For the first time we were all together in the same room.

Not all of us were that keen on sharing these anything but

spacious quarters. Tom Sutherland complained that the room was not big enough for all five of us to live in. But I was happy because of the opportunity to talk to and share with more people. David and Terry also seemed pleased by our new arrangement.

It hardly mattered what we thought though; we really had nothing to say about the matter. So on August 14, 1985, we five Americans became roommates. I was with these men until their release or mine.

Prior to Ben's and my arrival, Terry and David had a conversation with Hajj that went something like this: "We're not getting anywhere being held hostage. Your demands aren't even being heard. One of us has to be released to let the world know what's going on here and what your demands are."

Shortly after we all arrived in our basement prison, Hajj came in with an interpreter to tell us to choose someone to be released. He instructed us to vote for David Jacobson, Ben Weir, or me. We could not vote, however, for Terry Anderson or Tom Sutherland because they were spies.

Whether Hajj had intended it or not, giving us the responsibility for choosing who would be released turned out to be divisive and painful.

We prayed about it. I didn't feel I should be the first hostage released. "Really," I said, "the man who should go first is Ben Weir. He's the eldest. He has children and should go now." But Ben gently and generously said, "I don't wish to go either." That left David Jacobson. Yet we felt we needed someone out there who could reach the widest possible audience with our message. Because of his access to the media, Terry Anderson was the best candidate even though Hajj said not to vote for him. So we prayed some more.

We all agreed that our choice would have to be unanimous. After a number of ballots, the vote was four votes for Terry and one for David.

Although it was not unanimous I said, "That's it. Terry goes." In my religious community a unanimous vote always meant that all the votes were cast for the same person except one. No one votes for himself, so the person chosen would have voted for someone else.

Then Terry said, "No, Father, it's not unanimous." It took a moment for me to realize that, contrary to my assumption, someone other than Terry had voted for David and that Terry had voted for himself.

I was taken aback and strongly expressed my dismay to Terry because I never heard of anyone voting for themselves. Terry seemed really disturbed by what I said. He wanted to go badly, perhaps needed to go even more than the rest of us, as he was more unsettled, less certain in his life at the time of his kidnapping than the rest of us.

I think he knew, too, that he would probably have been the best spokesman for us. In the end, he was deeply saddened by what occurred. The two of us walked around the room and he was in tears. I had been harsh with him, perhaps not as much with words as with looks.

When Hajj returned we told him we had voted for Terry Anderson. His response was devastating. We should have been able to predict it. "Since you did not follow my directions, we are going to tell you who is going be released." Terry was upset by all that had happened and fell into an intense quarrel with David over why David had not supported him. It was a very painful, unhappy evening for all of us.

Nearly a month passed. September 14 is the Feast of the Exaltation of the Holy Cross, a feast the Christian communities in Lebanon celebrate with luminaria, small paper bags weighted with sand in which they place a lit candle and place outside in rows.

We had just finished celebrating Mass when Hajj came into the room and spoke to Ben Weir in Arabic. Blindfolded, we could all overhear the conversation but couldn't see them. We heard Ben respond with, "Oh my, oh my," and I was frightened for him. Once in the past after I had heard Ben say, "Oh my, oh my," he had been beaten.

But it was not bad news this time. It was good news. Hajj told him he was going to be released. Ben kept saying, "Oh my, oh my." It was a liberating thought—Ben going to freedom into that night of light, when the glow of candles was a familiar sight in the churches.

The guards let him shower and trimmed his hair. They gave him his clothes that he had washed earlier in the day. They were still damp. They allowed each one of us to write love letters to our families, which Ben carried out for us.

In the midst of all this, as Ben was getting himself together—I think he might have just finished tearing up the notes he'd been keeping through his months of captivity—Sayeed entered the room and said to me, "Abouna, we wanted you to go home. Why don't you go in Ben Weir's place?" I said nothing. I wished I hadn't heard him. I knew I would rather die than do anything to bring up the bitterness and demoralization we'd experienced concerning the question of who was to be released. I paid no attention to Sayeed and Ben was released within a few hours.

Ben was gone. The room was very quiet—a peculiar quiet. Our struggle had been futile. Our choice had been overruled. Hajj took it out of our hands. So there was quietness because it wasn't Terry or David, Martin or Tom. It was Ben. I sat in the corner, took a piece of cardboard I had saved, and wrote out the final scriptural passage we prayed that night before Ben left. As I wrote out the passage, I felt as if Ben was offering it to me, giving his farewell to Martin Jenco.

It comes from the letter of St. Paul to the Philippians, Chapter 4, verses 4 to 14. St. Paul (and Ben Weir) writes:

> Rejoice in the Lord always; again I will say, Rejoice. Let your gentleness be known to everyone. The Lord is near. Do not worry about anything, but in everything by prayer and supplication with thanksgiving let your requests be made known to God. And the peace of God, which surpasses all understanding, will guard your hearts and your minds in Christ Jesus.

Finally, beloved, whatever is true, whatever is honor-
able, whatever is just, whatever is pure, whatever is
pleasing, whatever is commendable, if there is any
excellence and if there is anything worthy of praise,
think about these things. Keep on doing the things
that you have learned and received and heard and
seen in me, and the God of peace will be with you.

I rejoice in the Lord greatly that now at last you have
revived your concern for me; indeed, you were concerned for me, but had no opportunity to show it.
Not that I am referring to being in need; for I have
learned to be content with whatever I have. I know
what it is to have little, and I know what it is to have
plenty. In any and all circumstances I have learned
the secret of being well-fed and of going hungry, of
having plenty and of being in need. I can do all
things through him who strengthens me. In any case,
it was kind of you to share my distress.

After Ben left, I would get depressed and need my spirits
uplifted. I'd pull out what had become Ben's letter to me and
read it, "Rejoice! Rejoice always in the Lord." It became sustenance to me. I personalized it, made it completely my own:

The Lord is near, Marty. Dismiss all anxiety from
your mind. Present your needs to God in every form
of prayer and in petitions full of gratitude.

And I did.

Then God's own peace, which is beyond all understanding, will stand guard over your heart and mind
in Christ Jesus.

And so it was.

After I read in St. Paul the exhortation, "Present your needs
to God in every form of prayer and in petitions full of gratitude,"
I searched scriptures to learn what my prayer was to be all about.

I found that I was to pray behind closed doors and in the presence of others; to be persistent and persevering in my prayer, to be thankful, and to believe that our prayers are really answered. I was to pray continually and never lose heart, to be quiet and patient and wait for the Lord.

I found, also, that I was to forgive. In Mark's gospel I read, "When you stand in prayer, forgive whatever you have against anybody, so that your Father in heaven may forgive your failings too (11:25, NJB)."

In the quietness of night when I was trying to fall asleep, I would hear the counsel of my brother Servite, Neal Flanagan, whom I loved greatly. I remembered Neal telling me, "Marty, if you want to see what hate does, you should go to Northern Ireland. Hate even changes your physical appearance."

Years before I read a book by Alan Paton, the famous South African author of *Cry, the Beloved Country*. He also wrote *The Instruments of Peace* based on the writings of St. Francis of Assisi. I remember reading something like this:

> I do not quite know why I do not hate my enemies. I know from experience that hate is corrosive and that one who hates does terrible damage to one's own character and personality. I can only thank God that I am not given to hating. What is more, I thank God for the knowledge that one becomes less and less given to hating as one becomes more and more given to loving.

It was very similar to what Neal Flanagan was saying—simply an attempt to live out the mandate of Jesus: "You have heard that it was said, 'You shall love your neighbor and hate your enemy.' But I say to you: Love your enemies and pray for those who persecute you" (Mt 5:43-44).

After Ben's release we were again moved to another location. In the middle of the night, they loaded us into a van and drove to another building in the southern suburbs of Beirut.

They told us to be very quiet going up the back stairs of this building. We walked up nine stories to the roof. Then we moved from this to the adjacent building, jumping the two foot space between rooftops.

As always, I was anxious. I remember sitting next to Terry after we arrived. The room looked relatively spacious. It did have a window—sealed, of course. But the room was clean. I experienced the usual expectations and hopes that we might be going home. Then Terry said, "It's not so bad. It's kind of nice." I thought, "Ugh. We've gotten to a dismal point—gauging the comparative 'niceness' of our prisons."

In a room right next to us were the French hostages and the Jewish doctor our captors had kidnapped to look after us. One of the French hostages, named Michel Seurat, was extremely ill and near death. The doctor was very alarmed and after Seurat died, we never saw the doctor again. Some of the prisoners heard a gunshot once the doctor left Seurat's room. I later found out that the doctor had been executed. After my release I met his wife in France, and although she asked why her husband had been killed, she did not have a look of hate in her eyes. I think she understood it takes an eternity for an answer. I would also meet Seurat's wife and at the time she was very hateful of her husband's captors.

We knew that Ben would be working tirelessly to secure our release, that he would be doing all he could to focus media attention on the plight of his brother hostages. We began insisting to our captors that we should be appraised of Ben's efforts so that we could counsel them on what helpful actions they might take. In short, we needed access to radio, newspaper, television—any source of information.

We also told them that we should be writing to certain powerful and influential persons. We especially hoped those who received our letters could urge President Reagan to engage in something more than "quiet diplomacy," a process through which diplomats were working for our release on humanitarian grounds.

We experienced no small measure of delight when Hajj responded by giving us access to the radio and newspaper and permitted us to write letters. It gave us a sense of some power in working out our destinies. Hope acquired a more active meaning for us. We used the radio from the end of September to February. Later Hajj took the radio away because he did not want us to hear any bad news.

The guards brought us a magazine called "Monday Morning," or something like that. I remember reading an article in which a Syrian general, a close friend of the actress Gina Lollobrigida, commented that the hostage situation would quickly be remedied and we would soon be free. Nothing happened, and every time I saw his name in the paper, his words echoed in my mind. It was just like the guards saying, "Soon, soon you're going to go home." Just to look at the man's picture made me angry because I knew his words were empty of any substance.

Our radio was a small Sony that we shared with the Frenchmen. Getting it back and forth between the two hostage groups required the guards to act as middlemen. When the Frenchmen wanted it, we had to give it to them; and when we wanted it, they had to give it to us. It became a bone of contention because the guards did not want to be disturbed from their eating, sleeping, or watching television. Eventually we worked out a schedule.

We listened primarily to the BBC and the Voice of America. We found the BBC generally more informative, but both were important sources of news for us.

We learned from the Voice of America and newspaper sources that two Republican congressmen were always speaking on our behalf—George O'Brien from Will County, Illinois, the location of Joliet; and Robert Dornan from David Jacobson's home county of Orange in California. Every day they entered our names in the Congressional Record and reminded other legislators of our plight. We asked if we could write to thank these men and ask them to continue to remind government officials of our situation, and to pressure President Reagan to move beyond quiet diplomacy. Later I discovered that Congressman O'Brien traveled to Damascus and petitioned the Syrian government to intervene on our behalf. He died a few days prior to my release, so I never had a chance to thank him and to share my joy with him.

Hajj, at our insistence, allowed us to write letters to President Reagan, Archbishop of Canterbury Robert Runcie, the two congressmen, and the Associated Press and other media.

Access to a radio was very strange after having been cut off from any sense of actively participating in the outside world for months. Tom Sutherland brought us our last news when he joined us in July, and it was a month old. Suddenly we had the world as a visitor who came and went on a regular schedule. We were always anxious to hear news and to get back in touch with social and political realities.

We heard one news item claiming that the Islamic Jihad had killed all of us. We were allowed to write letters to our families to prove this claim to be nothing more than a sick hoax.

During this time, two unique things occurred. One night the guards either forgot to give, or would not give, the radio to the French hostages. So in the middle of the night I tuned in Voice of America. I was astonished to hear a familiar voice. My nephew John Jenco was speaking to me! It was such a shocker in the darkness, in the quiet of the cell, to hear my nephew encouraging me to hang on.

Some days later I turned on the Voice of America again and caught an interview with John Donahue, who'd been my CRS boss in Thailand. He spoke about his new position in Gambia, Africa, and what CRS was doing there. It stirred profound emotions in me to hear his voice, too.

We also tried to catch *Prairie Home Companion* as a way of staying in touch with home. But we listened to non-American and non-English programs, too. One night Tom Sutherland tuned in a French-language program. We had just heard on the Voice of America that the U.S. space shuttle Challenger was due to lift off. I was sitting on my mat next to Tom when suddenly he put the radio down, saying, "The Challenger exploded on take-off." In shock, I said to him, "Tom, I don't want to hear that. I just don't want to hear that." The thought of such a tragedy was too much for me to handle.

Through the day, we tried to get Voice of America but there was very little on. Finally came the new reports: it was true, the Challenger had indeed exploded. An anchorman was sharing his experience of the lift-off and explosion, of seeing the parents of the school teacher, Sharon Christa McAuliffe. He said, "If anything communicates the meaning of this tragedy, it's the look of the mother and father at the moment of that explosion." Later I saw it on videotape: the lift-off, the explosion, the look of Christa's mother and father as they turned to each other. And it was true. Their look said everything.

The event stands out in my memory because we didn't want to hear bad news. It received lots of press and became very much a part of our daily conversations. Now when I see film clips or references to the event, I am taken back to my prison.

Occasionally the guards let us, or—depending on how one feels about these things—forced us to watch television. As with other activities that seemed merely routine before our capture, it became an altogether unique experience because of the conditions created by the guards. We had to sit very close to the screen—something attentive parents would not permit their children to do. The guards sat behind us, cradling automatic weapons—something attentive children would not permit their parents to do. We were not allowed to look back at them. You might not even look away from the screen because they might think you were starting to look back at them.

This exquisite form of torture involved our being compelled to watch soap operas like *Dallas*, *Knott's Landing*, and other programs of that caliber. You can imagine the devastating effect this had on us. Afterward, we found ourselves actually discussing these programs. Tom Sutherland would get the characters mixed up or transpose an incident from one program to the other.

Actually it all provided rather lively entertainment—in contrast to what we had experienced at the hands of these remorseless gunmen.

From the BBC we learned that the Archbishop of Canterbury, Robert Runcie, had contacted Ben Weir and offered to work for our release through his envoy and troubleshooter Terry Waite. Waite had had some negotiation successes, specifically securing the release of British hostages in Iran and Lybia. Aware of these successes, this announcement was cause for optimism. We asked Hajj if we could write to the Archbishop thanking him for his concern and care, and requesting that Terry Waite be our mediator.

On Christmas Eve day the BBC announced Terry Waite's arrival in Lebanon. Even before this news, Terry had been in touch with our captors. In order to make sure he was dealing with people who had access to us, he gave them a Polaroid camera and a copy of that day's *London Times* with his name written across the top. We were then photographed holding that newspaper. This not only demonstrated he was dealing with our captors, but helped quash new rumors that we had been executed or had died in captivity.

To be sure, our hopes and expectations skyrocketed with the thought we might be released for Christmas. Each of us had his own idea of what it would be like when he got out and of what he would do first. Terry would go immediately to his fiancée Madeleine's place in Beirut. Tom wanted to go back to the American University in Beirut, take a couple days rest, and resume his teaching responsibilities.

I kept saying, "It's not going to work that way. They're not going to allow that. You should think differently." Nevertheless, we all had our own expectations.

Mine was simply to be dropped off somewhere in Beirut. I'd walk into a hotel and call home to let my family know I was free and I would be home shortly. My dream was always just to walk through the back door of my sister's place in Joliet and say, "Hi!

I'm home." In the end, that dream would prove just as unreal as I had thought Tom's and Terry's.

On Christmas Eve night we got the radio back from the Frenchmen to catch any late-breaking news. The news that broke, broke our hearts. We heard that Waite had faltered in his negotiations and would return to London to spend Christmas with his family. He left promising to return. Apparently he needed to do other things before our release could be realized.

We marked the passage from Advent to Christmas—from the season of hopeful expectation to the season of fulfillment—with Midnight Mass. To illumine our little cell, we lit what candles we had. Outside, tremendous shelling split the night. We tried, our hopes all in ruins, to celebrate the birth of Jesus, the Servant of Peace.

St. Paul writes in his letter to the Romans that when you can't find ways to speak to God, the Holy Spirit sighs on your behalf. That night we heard the sigh of the Holy Spirit in each man's pain, each wanting one simple, but impossible thing—to be home with his loved ones at Christmas.

Most of us knew Christmas carols by heart. But when we tried to sing, our voices would crack. Memories of other Christmases bounced in and out of our minds constantly. That Christmas attained a special place in our memories, too.

On Christmas Day they moved us to the end room of the apartment house saying we would be safer there from the violence wrecking the day—and so many lives.

The guards also did something quite astonishing. First they gave us special food—chicken and pickles and other Lebanese food the likes of which we hadn't seen in months. Then they brought us together, set something they wanted us to see on the floor, and allowed us to lift our blindfolds a little. There we saw a beautiful cake with candles flaming and "Happy Birthday Jesus" written on top. One of the young guards sang a highly-accented rendition of "Happy Birthday, Jesus." We hadn't tasted anything sweet like that in a long time.

The young guards, I believe, really wanted us to go home,

too, and they themselves were disappointed that negotiations had failed to bring about our release. I suspect that the men who had kidnapped us didn't share much information with these young men, except to give them orders on how to look after us. I don't think our guards were included in the decision-making process when it came to more significant matters.

They allowed us to write love letters to our families that day. I wondered what I should tell my family about my little corner of the world. I just couldn't let them know what this was all about. Why should I contribute any more to their worry? So I simply wrote:

Dear brothers and sisters,

If I am to die, I hope that I would die with the words of Jesus on my lips: "Father, forgive them; for they do not know what they are doing." Please do not hate them and if you want to know where I am spiritually, read Psalms 116, 117, and 118.

Much love,
Larry

CHAPTER NINE

SEEING CHRIST IN ONE ANOTHER

But, Lord remember me and mine
Wi mercies temp'ral and devine,
That I for gear and grace may shine
Excell'd by nane,
And a' the glory shall be thine,
Amen, Amen!

—*Holy Willie's Prayer*
Robert Burns

Our days passed in ritualistic repetition. We would use the toilet, wash our clothes, and shower all in our morning visit to the bathroom in this last of my prisons. After a while, it became an almost unconscious routine that I could pretty well complete in the time allotted. Sometimes I'd do it even faster. I don't know why—perhaps because I knew some of the other men needed more time and got in trouble as a result.

The guards didn't like waiting for us. They'd knock on the door of our room and say, "Who's ready to go to the toilet?" I'd get angry because who's ready to go at the snap of someone else's fingers? We'd wait until someone would say, "I'll go."

Sometimes I'd go first. Other times I thought, "I'm not going to say I'll go first today. I'm going to see if someone else offers to go first." It's the sort of thing you naturally resist, going to the toilet at someone else's command.

When my turn came I'd gather my dirty clothes—that is, what I had on—plus urine bottle, clean clothes, soap, toothpaste, toothbrush, and stand in front of the door until they opened it. I had to look down beneath my blindfold past the bundle of personal gear I was carrying as I walked along the corridor to the toilet.

Then I would set everything down and fill my water bottle from the sink. Even though the guards said we shouldn't drink it, I always did. Then I'd empty the urine bottle and wash my clothes and take a shower.

Sometimes the water was frigid. Sometimes it was hot. When it was frigid I'd shower in a second, only long enough to get the grime off. Sometimes the water was so cold it hurt. Then I would have to wait, knock on the door and say, "I'm ready to go." A guard would come, take me back to the room, and then the next guy would go. It was that kind of a ritual.

There was always the dream that one day we would be free and we would find out where we had been held. Sometimes when I went to the toilet I would stand on the commode and look out the window trying to figure out where I was. I knew I was somewhere in the southern suburbs of Beirut because I could hear the planes coming and going from the airport.

I'm not sure now if I could identify the buildings. But as a hostage, I had this desire: "One day I'm going to identify this place." It's perhaps similar to the desire of survivors of the Nazi concentration camps or the WWII prison of war camps to go back and look around.

I'm sure the guards didn't want anybody to know we were there, but they would take us out blindfolded onto the balcony to expose us to some sunlight. When the guards weren't around I would peek around to see what I could see.

Sometimes a young guard named Fadl was on duty. Fadl was a curious man. The other guards harassed and made fun of him.

But when Fadl was on in the early morning, he would come in and bring us Turkish coffee. It was such a treat. The only person who didn't drink the coffee was Tom Sutherland. I never understood why, but it was an extra cup of coffee for us to share.

Fadl would come into the darkness of our room. The lights from the corridor would shine on him and I could see completely through my blindfold and make out his face.

He'd pour the coffee into the cups placed on our floor. I'd always pat his back and say, "Thank you, Fadl. I really appreciate this." He knew that I was really stroking him, affirming him for kindness, something he needed because of his treatment by his fellow guards. I suppose I needed it too.

We had many conversations with the guards. We discussed religion, politics, the need to love and be loved, mothers and fathers, wives and marriage, children, health—all normal topics in an abnormal setting.

We each had one guard we preferred over another; and I believe they felt the same about us. The guards would even pick up on our emotional state, be it boredom, anger, or sadness. They would find my silence annoying. A passive, nonviolent response would irritate them into silence. I really believe they wanted to be my friends. Strangely they wanted approval for their acts of kindness and their acts of cruelty.

One day Abu Ali asked me, "Abouna, teach me what Jesus has to say about love." Through our conversations, a mutual realization of each other's dreams was gradually transforming two enemies into brothers.

Sayeed once gave us a list of all the evils: certain foods (mainly pork), music, dress, art, and many others I can't recall. At the end of his list I asked if kidnapping was not an evil. His shout was one of silence.

The guards got days off. Sayeed would go home and then bring back his daughter and son to our cell without fear for their safety. Occasionally friends of the guards would visit them. By peeking I would catch them sneaking a look at their caged human animals.

After our experience with the Christmas cake, David Jacobson got the idea of telling the guards, "It's the anniversary of Father Jenco's priesthood. We should give him a special meal and a cake." The guards honored that, actually making a special meal and purchasing a cake. My American brothers in captivity and the guards helped me celebrate my twenty-seventh anniversary as a priest.

And so it went—"It's Father Jenco's feast day," or, "It's Father Jenco's birthday," or "It's David's birthday," and any anniversaries we could think of. On those occasions the guards would purchase a special cake. Then Tom's birthday came and they gave him cupcakes and candles. Tom complained, "Well, how come Father Jenco gets cake and I only get cupcakes?" I chuckled. We were very grateful to get cupcakes.

On some occasions, such as the anniversary of my ordination, the other hostages would ask what it was all about. And I would ask questions about their families, their marriages, their celebrations, and how their families got together. It was always so beautiful to share each other's stories.

I was ordained on Easter Monday. The gospel reading for our anniversary eucharist that day tells of the journey to Emmaus. Two followers of Jesus are walking to Emmaus, depressed and saddened by the fact that their Messiah had been killed. Jesus catches up with them and asks, "What are all these things that you are discussing as you walk along?" Not recognizing him, they tell him, "You must be the only person staying in Jerusalem who does not know the things that have been happening there these last few days." The man they thought was to be the Messiah was killed. Now they heard that he had arisen from the dead. As Jesus walked along with them he opened their minds to the scriptures and shared with them the passages about who this Messiah is.

They walked along on their journey and God unveiled himself. They're touched, and they glow with this experience. They press Jesus to stay with them and he sits down at table with them. They didn't recognize him in the opening of the scriptures, but they recognize him in the breaking of the bread.

I found that to be very significant: we recognize the Christ in the breaking of bread. In captivity I came to recognize Christ in the others in just our simple breaking of bread. I would use that to uplift me and to sustain me as a hostage.

We continued to look for occasions to celebrate. During the month of May, the only big celebration I recalled was Mother's Day. None of our mothers were alive, but all were very important to us. In June I celebrated my mother's birthday and we celebrated Father's Day. Terry Anderson and David Jacobson's fathers were still living. David had the glorious opportunity to hug his dad once again upon his release. My dad had died when I was a teenager, and one joy I wished I had known in life was to know him as an adult. In the course of these days, insights into our parents were very, very important.

In July we celebrated the Fourth. On the Fourth of July the previous year, CRS called from New York asking me to go to Beirut as Program Director. July also brought the Feast of Our Lady of Mount Carmel. One of my first assignments as a young priest was to Our Lady of Mount Carmel parish in Denver, located in a neighborhood called "Little Italy."

The feast brought back pleasant memories of my time there. They had really spoiled me. The parish celebrated the feasts of St. Rocco and Our Lady of Mount Carmel. On both days it would have a bazaar with a procession meandering through the neighborhood, a band, and good Italian food. During the procession, the statue of Our Lady of Mount Carmel was draped with a cloth stole on which people would pin money. These were wonderful gatherings of Italians from all over the city who came to celebrate their favorite feast days.

The lack of variety in my diet caused me still another period of food obsession. I started dreaming about pickled herring again. I would eat everything, even orange and lemon rinds. One morning at the end of Ramadan the guards brought in a purple soup made of lamb hooves. It was pure, liquid barnyard—and an act of aromatic terrorism—but I held my nose and I drank it, believing this was what they themselves were eating. Sometimes food was scarce and the young guards had to eat hostage fare, too. I think Terry Anderson was the only other hostage who ate it. The other two couldn't.

That afternoon a guard came in and I felt something drop into my lap. I looked down beneath the lower edge of my blindfold and saw the cooked head of a lamb, eyes and all, staring up at me. I was honestly shocked. I told the young guard, "I cannot eat that." He asked, "Why ever not?" I was used to arguing with the guards to the point of exasperation in order to maintain whatever boundaries I could. But this time—I believe, under most genuine inspiration—I didn't argue. Like a formula I uttered "It's haram—against my religion." Without so much as a question or hesitation he picked it up and walked out saying "Oh, I'm sorry." The other hostages asked, "What was it, Marty?"

"It was the head of a lamb and I just couldn't eat it," I responded.

And they started to laugh and said, "Well, your response was so instant, you know. 'It's against my religion. I cannot eat it.'"

Terry Anderson fashioned a deck of cards out of paper scraps from magazines and books, which provided us another way to occupy ourselves. We played Hearts relentlessly. Terry seemed to win a little too often and I felt like I was his favorite victim for dumping the Queen of Spades. So when he was out of the room going to the toilet one morning I said, "We really should work together against him." I was able to dump the Queen of Spades on him. Terry got very angry and said, "You're so vindictive!" And I said, "Terry, this is a card game. It's meant to be vindictive." We were becoming truly adept in the art of creative purgation.

Sometimes we had to hide our cards when the guards came in. Then we'd forget whose turn it was, what cards were played, who had the queen, and the like. Ordinarily, we didn't welcome the coming of the guards, but there were occasions, particularly

when I was losing badly, that I didn't mind it so much. The inter-
rupted game would have to be started again.

We also played Twenty Questions. When my turn came to
pick a subject, I chose the Smoo from the comic strip *Lil' Abner.*
The first question was "Is it animal, vegetable, or mineral." The
Smoo was whatever you wanted it to be. I loved it. When the
questions came too close to identifying the Smoo, I'd change
what it was. I won that round.

David Jacobson read tea leaves after our morning tea. First
he'd read his own and then he'd read mine. I'd always chuckle
because the readings were so positive. The tea leaves always
spoke of being delivered, getting out of there, being present to
my family, flying over the west or east coast of the United States.

Tom Sutherland treated us to exceptional recitations of the
poetry of Robert Burns. He was a well known reciter of Burns'
poetry even as a young person, and later as a professor at
Colorado State University. He toured Colorado, giving his
recitals in a kilt. He was particularly in demand on the feast of
St. Andrew, the patron saint of Scotland.

Some of those poems—"To a Louse" and "Holy Willie's
Prayer"— touched me greatly, and Tom's interpretations would
always lift my spirits. I would say, "Tom, do you remember that
poem, you know. Would you mind repeating it for me?" For most
of my captivity, whenever things turned crazy, I'd ask Tom to
recite some poetry for me and he always responded so graciously.

The guards told us we should exercise to become body
beautifuls for our wives and women. They would remove our
chains so we could do push-ups. I didn't need that. They were
too painful and I told the others I would not do any push-ups
until the day of my release. Then I would only do one—for sym-
bolic reasons.

Occasionally they would take us out of our room. They
would give us phrases in Arabic, probably some sort of religious
formulae, and then march us back and forth along the corridor.
I remember Terry Anderson telling the guards he would not do
it. I regarded it as an opportunity to get out of that sealed room.

If that's what it took, I would march up and down and shout whatever they wanted. At least there was some sunlight in the corridor.

Basically I exercised when we put our mats against the wall and walked in a circle around the room. I didn't even care to run in place when we had our chains on. Terry would tell the others that "Father is so lazy his watch won't wind."

When we would walk around the room we would lead each other on different journeys. On one occasion David walked us mentally along a beach in southern California, then gave us a tour of the nearby highways, byways, and alleyways. Terry took us on a walking tour of Tokyo. I gave a tour of Rome, including its ancient monuments, various basilicas, St. Peter's, the Sistine Chapel, and the Vatican Museum. I ended up at the Servite monastery of San Marcello where we had an Italian meal: it began with a glass of vermouth and an antipasto, proceeded to soup and spaghetti, then to the main course with both ordinary wine and *vino speciale*, culminating with dessert and a liqueur. Then came an afternoon siesta. It was a wonderful way of walking for hours in a circle. Each of us occupied worlds much larger than our nine-by-twelve-foot room.

Terry Anderson made rosaries out of string. He and I were the only Catholics, but Terry taught Dave and Tom how to use it. It was always interesting to watch. Occasionally I'd see them finger their rosary and pray.

The fighting caused frequent power outages. Sometimes our only light for hours came from the flame of a single candle. We used candles very sparingly because we couldn't be sure the guards would replenish our supply. Whenever I'd blow one out, I would cup my hand just above it to catch the fragrant smoke, and say, "Dear God, let my prayer rise like incense before you."

When it rained, the roof leaked and we would have water all over the room. Our mats got wet and smelly. We'd then ask the guards, "Please take them out into the sun to dry," and they would. When that happened we had a lot more space in the room which was nice.

We also had clean-up days. Terry was very finicky about being clean. The guards allowed us to paint the room one day, but the paint was awfully drab. Every prison apartment I lived in was battleship gray. I wondered why. Perhaps it was the cheapest paint available. But battleship gray? A little splash of color would have been nice.

During this period in what was my last prison we were allowed to keep journals. I would try to write every day. After a while there was not much to write about because the daily ritual didn't change much. Sometimes I'd record a passage from a book I was reading or something that happened to me that day—like Hajj coming into the room. I also recorded things I heard on the BBC.

With Ben Weir's farewell, and believing that forgiveness was the heart of love, I decided to annoy my guards with love. Strangely, I wondered about my love for my fellow hostages. One difficult day, after being sealed in a room for twenty-four hours with only a fifteen minute exit to use the toilet, I wrote in my journal, "Oh God, I am so glad I'm not married to any of these men."

When you live with three men in the same room for almost a year, you're bound to get on each others' nerves. We learned the bad and the good of each other. There were times that accentuated the ugly as well as the wonderful. It sounded like marriage.

When I got out of captivity and met their wives and families, I asked, "Were they always that way?" and they said, "Yes."

Tom Sutherland used to tell me that he's only this way because of being held hostage but when I met his wife and daughters, they said, "Oh dad's always been that way." As a male in a household with four women Tom complained that they used too much tissue. As hostages toilet paper and tissue was rationed. Sharing it drove him absolutely crazy and he would squirrel it away.

I know, too, that at times I was cruel to my brother hostages. They can excuse or forgive me because of the situation but sometimes I find myself saying, "I need to tell him that I'm sorry that I said that." But that's part of the human condition. We get caught up situations that seem unendurable. Somehow we have to accept both our holiness and our sinfulness.

I often wondered if any of the others ever cried. I certainly did. Sometimes in the evening when the lights were out and people were asleep I would secretly cry. Perhaps it was out of boredom, or frustration, or longing. One of these days I'll be able to ask these men, "Did you ever cry?" And I am sure they will tell me, "Yes, I cried."

I complained to God, "Listen, I am not Job. I want to go home now." I would ask God "Why this," and "Why am I here?" I thought perhaps I hadn't worked hard enough in the refugee camps, where men, women, and children were imprisoned for years while I was free to walk in and out at will. Finally, I realized that God doesn't work that way.

As a hostage, I only wanted one thing: to go home. One particularly torturous game they played with us resulted in great psychological pain. Three times they brought us clothes—a pair of pants, shirt, shoes, and socks. They said, "You have to change into these clothes. You're going home. You have to wait just a little now." We would change clothes and wait—our expectations precisely that we were to be released. I would find myself filled to bursting with all kinds of joy.

A couple of hours later they would come back and say, "We're just kidding." The first time they did that, I wept silently. The guards were talking, and then were suddenly quiet. They could see the tears dropping from beneath the blindfold to the floor. I don't think they handled tears very well.

When they moved us out of the bedroom with the sealed windows to a room at the end of the corridor we heard hammering and banging. I had this fantastic sense that I was going to be released. But when they took me back to the bedroom and I lifted my blindfold, I saw what the hammering was about: another door had been hung on the jamb, like a screen door, with the room door. Only this one was like a gate made with bars—indicating that it would be a long time before we'd be leaving that place. I just let the tears fall.

Sayeed saw the tears dropping to the floor and said, "Oh no! What's wrong?" I said, "Sayeed, you keep telling me that I'm going to go home and I know what you put on this room. Another door, a sealed door with bars. That tells me I am not going home."

"No, no," he said. "It's only that we have to give you air because we could not leave your door open." They had hung the door with bars so that the solid door could be left open and allow us some circulation.

There had been no air in there. Some nights were so hot that I would lie on the floor near the door, hoping for the coolness of the cement and the air from beneath the door to help me cope with the heat.

I dreamt of going home day and night, sleeping and waking. One dream recurred quite frequently. I would be kneeling at my mother's and father's graves in Joliet. As I knelt I heard the sound of wooden chimes. Eerie, since, actually, there were none there.

When I returned to Joliet after my release, I went to the cemetery and knelt at my mom's and dad's graves. They were among the saints I had petitioned to intercede before God on my behalf that I might go free. I thanked them and remembering my recurrent dream as a hostage, hung a set of wooden chimes in the branches of a tree nearby.

CHAPTER TEN

SIGHS TOO DEEP FOR WORDS

The Lord looked down from his holy height,
from heaven he beheld the earth,
to hear the groans of the prisoners,
to set free those who were doomed to die.
                              —Psalm 102:19-20

Saint Paul in his letter to the Romans writes:

> Likewise the Spirit helps us in our weakness; for we
> do not know how to pray as we ought, but that very
> Spirit intercedes with sighs too deep for words. And
> God, who searches the heart, knows what is the
> mind of the Spirit, because the Spirit intercedes for
> the saints according to the will of God (8:26-27).

At times our physical groans and sighs were so loud it was
as if the Spirit was speaking through us, sighing on our behalf.
We'd ask God to be attentive to us, to hear our sighs, groans, and
cries, the prayers of our hearts, the heaviness we could not find
words to relieve. We would listen to the pain of each other
through our sighs and groans, knowing that sometimes the
words could not be found.

One of the three letters I received as a hostage came from Sister
Bernadine, a Sister of Mercy with whom I had worked in Australia.
While I was there, she ran a home for alcoholic aboriginal men,

women, and children in downtown Perth. Now she worked with prisoners.

She wrote that the prisoners were praying for my release, knowing I was being held unjustly. It reminded me of the gospel story of the two criminals crucified next to Jesus; the one tells the other not to taunt Jesus because they were being justly punished while Jesus was not.

Their letter referred to Psalm 102, which is a prayer in a time of distress, in which the afflicted one cries out:

> Hear my prayer, O Lord;
> let my cry come to you.
> Do not hide not your face from me
> in the day of my distress.
> Incline your ear to me;
> answer me speedily in the day when I call.
> For my days pass away like smoke,
> and my bones burn like a furnace. . . .
> Let this be recorded for a generation to come,
> so that a people yet unborn may praise the Lord:
> that he looked down from his holy height,
> from heaven the the Lord looked at the earth,
> to hear the groans of the prisoners,
> to set free those who were doomed to die.

For most of us, the book of Psalms was a source of great consolation. Certain words and phrases of our unveiling God became embedded in our hearts, minds, and souls:

> For great is his steadfast love toward us,
> and the faithfulness of the Lord endures forever
> (117:2).

> His steadfast love endures forever (118:4).

> I believe that I shall see the goodness of the Lord
> in the land of the living.
> Wait for the Lord;
> be strong, and let your heart take courage;

wait for the Lord (27:13-14)!

Let them thank the Lord for his steadfast love,
for his wonderful works to humankind.
And let them offer thanksgiving sacrifices,
and tell of his deeds with songs of joy (107:21-22).

The Hebrew and Christian covenants became our assurance
that God was with us, unveiling the story of God's faithful presence to his people. The more we entered into these covenants, the
more we discerned the way they made sense of our own lives.

Scriptures became a marvelous love story of our gentle
God. In the Hebrew covenant God constantly speaks of his loving faithfulness toward all, even though we are not faithful to the
covenant of love. It is as if God is saying, "I love you, I love you,"
and at one point says, "I will no longer speak the word 'love.' I
will send Love Incarnate, Jesus the Christ."

In the Christian covenant, the more we recognize who Jesus
is, the more we see God's loving presence, power, and plan in our
own lives and especially in our horrendous situation. We prayed
that the God of covenant-promises would continue to work
through us in spite of the chains, blindfolds, brutality, threats,
death, loneliness, and sense of abandonment on our pilgrimage
home.

Our discussions of scripture were not without humor. One
evening I was conducting our prayer service and we read the
chapters from Genesis on Sodom and Gomorrah. In my reflec-
tion I stated that whenever we think of the great wickedness of
these cities, we immediately think of sins of the flesh. I asked,
"What about pride, gluttony, idleness, heartlessness, and the
infringement of the most sacred laws of hospitality?" But our
shared homily didn't dwell on these. It refocused on a discussion
of homosexuality. At the close of our prayer service, David
Jacobson commented that he couldn't "wait to get out of here to
hear a good sermon."

I read scripture I don't know how many times, with many

unanswerable questions resulting from my captivity. The other hostages also had questions that I just could not respond to. New and old mysteries seemed to converge.

It was reminiscent of Mary and Joseph's finding Jesus in the Temple, after several days' search. He responds to their frantic questioning by asking: "Why were you looking for me? Did you not know I must be in my Father's house?" Mary and Joseph didn't understand what he was saying but his mother "stored up all these things in her heart." So it was for me as a hostage. The reading of God's word was sometimes so mysterious and difficult to comprehend, I had to keep all these things in my heart and know that God would one day unveil their meanings fully.

I really wanted to walk through my scripture readings with brother Servite and New Testament professor Neal Flanagan when I got out. I often felt him and his counsel in some of my darkest nights as a hostage. I hoped to collaborate with him on a book and incorporate this walk through the scriptures. But when I learned of his death after my release, all desire to write died.

Easter 1986 was celebrated in the company of my hostage brothers Terry, David, and Tom. For our Palm Sunday procession I blessed some stems saved from oranges to use as palms. Through the week, we each took turns reading the passion stories in the gospels of Matthew, Mark, and Luke. We read with deep feeling, evoking powerful emotions in each other. On Holy Thursday we celebrated the institution of the sacraments of priesthood and eucharist. On Good Friday we again read one of the passion accounts. On Holy Saturday I blessed some water in a little cup as the waters of baptism. A candle I salvaged served as our Paschal Candle. With these we then celebrated the midnight Easter Vigil.

On Easter Day Abu Ali, the young guard who had always been gentle to me and who had once asked me to teach him what Jesus had to say about love, said, "Abouna, may I come to your Easter Mass?" I said, "Yes." If he came, it meant that we would have to celebrate our Easter Day Mass blindfolded. I had spent my first Easter as a hostage blindfolded and chained to a wall. I had hoped to spend this one with my sight free. But I said yes, and he came.

Throughout these times, we sang the gospel acclamation "Allelu! Allelu! Everyone sing Allelu! For the Lord is risen, it is true. Everyone sing Allelu!"

During the day, I thought I heard my young Muslim brother singing "Allelu!" and all I could do was smile. Then in the afternoon I heard the door open. We were blindfolded, but I could feel someone come over and kneel down next to me where I was sitting on the floor. Something was laid in my lap. I looked down beneath my blindfold. A bouquet of flowers! Abu Ali whispered in my ear, "Abouna, happy Easter!" There will never be another choir like our Alleluia choir, and there will never be another bouquet like that Easter bouquet. None of us had seen flowers in a year, more than that in my case.

And what beauty there is in a flower!

Sometime in June '86 each hostage made a videotape that was to be given to the United States government. Each tape was broken into two segments: in the first we spoke to our families; in the second, to the United States government. Our captors brought in a camera crew for the purpose. We were not supposed to look at the crew members, which was almost impossible. We had to stare and speak only into the cameras.

We could say basically anything we wanted to our families—and they could see that we were in good health. We spoke about our daily routine, things such as that. But we could say nothing negative about the physical condition of our prison. Only good things. Consequently, little was said on that subject.

Our captors provided the script for the part directed to the U.S. government. It basically stated the following:

> That they (our captors) were very sorry they kidnapped us, but they believed it was the only effective means of letting the American people know our policy in the Middle East was basically pro-Israel and that we did not listen to Arab voices. That because the

United States government subsidized Israel with bil-
lions of dollars, it thereby collaborated with Israel's
invasion of Lebanon and is equally responsible for the
tremendous destruction visited on Lebanon. That
when the United States government sent Marines as a
peace-keeping force into Lebanon, the U.S. did not
remain neutral, but sided with the Gemayel regime
which was interested primarily in perpetuating the
heavy-handed Christian Phalangists' domination
rather than sharing power with the Muslims as provided by the Lebanese constitution.

The script also pointed out that when the Marine barracks
were destroyed by the car bomb that killed so many Marines, the
U.S. retaliated with indiscriminate bombing and shelling of
Lebanese mountain villages. The inhabitants included people of
diverse politics and religions. In an act of senseless violence,
men, women, and children were killed who had nothing to do
with the attack on the Marines. If there were to be retaliation, it
should have been against those who attacked the Marines.

In the tape to my family, I did slip in a negative—that my
teeth were very bad. They felt like chalk. Once before I had asked
Hajj for a dentist because my teeth were so painful. All he said
was, "Perhaps." Even the fillings Sayeed said were transmitters
began to fall out. So now I told my family that if ever I got out
of here I'd need to see a dentist.

Not long after, they pulled me out of the cell and sat me
blindfolded in a chair. Someone said, "Open your mouth." A
dentist, whom I believe was kidnapped, injected me with a local
anesthetic. He was preparing to pull a tooth which had lost its
filling and was causing me extreme pain. I reacted very strangely for me. I fainted. My keepers got very excited, moving me to
another room and cooling me off with the fan. When I came to,
the dentist said, "I could care less if you see me." So I was
allowed to take off my blindfold. He was a very young man and
very competent. He pulled the tooth, sutured it properly, and
gave me some antibiotics to prevent infection.

The other men had also mentioned in their taping sessions that their teeth were going bad and that they would need to see a dentist. When I returned to our quarters I sat next to Tom Sutherland who asked, "Well, what happened?" and I said, "They pulled my tooth." And as soon as I finished those very words, the door opened. The guards came in with the dentist, who went to all three men, one at a time, asking them about the condition of their teeth. I heard each man reply, "My teeth are fine." I started to laugh because I knew that their teeth were not fine but they were afraid they would have to have a tooth pulled.

In the midst of all this, an intuition came to me. I was surprised that they were suddenly concerned about my teeth. Then came a gut feeling. I was going home soon. Leaning against the wall one day, praying and reading scriptures, I'd repeatedly come across the passage in Psalms, "Trust in the Lord. Wait for the Lord." It echoed continually in my mind, "Trust in the Lord. Wait for the Lord. You're going to be going home soon." This utter trust that I would soon go home upheld me powerfully.

On July 26 Hajj came in with Ali the interpreter to tell us we were being moved. It was a hot July morning, especially so in a sealed ninth floor room. It was unhealthy and they told us we were going to a healthier place. Once again our anxiety level skyrocketed.

They told us to take only our clothes and gave us little plastic bags in which to pack those we weren't wearing. We were not allowed to take books, notes, our urine bottle or water bottle. Then they instructed us in a very formal procedure for leaving. Dressed and blindfolded we were to proceed, one at a time, to the elevator. We were to board the elevator, and then remove our blindfolds. We were to exit at the ground floor and then walk briskly outside to a waiting van, get in and put our blindfolds back on. Five minutes would elapse between each person's departure from our room.

The key slid into the lock on the cell door. Someone said, "David, come." David got up wearing his blindfold and carrying his little bag, and left the room. Five minutes later, the sound of the key, then, "Tom, you come." And Tom left with his little bag. The last two persons in the room were Terry and I. The departure anxiety was very intense by now. We were just sharing a few moments together when we heard the key in the lock. We both pulled our blindfolds back down over our eyes and stood up. They instructed me to sit down and said, "Terry Anderson, you come." I walked over to Terry and I gave him a hug and a kiss. I said, "Goodbye, Terry."

"Why are you saying goodbye?" he asked.

I answered, "Well, I'm not too sure I'm going to be in the same prison with you, so—just in case—goodbye." And Terry left.

Five minutes later the key went into the door and I stood up. They said, "Abouna, we told you to sit down." I sat down. I was staring at the floor and I said to Hajj, "Hajj, are you going to kill me?"

Hajj replied, "No, Abouna, you are going to go home now." I started to cry. The rule was we were not allowed to cry, but Hajj responded to my tears. He said, "Now, I'm beginning to understand tears." They became quiet and honored my tears.

They closed the door to the room again, effectively sealing it, so that I was unable to get any fresh air. It was very hot so I knocked on the door and asked, "Would you please leave the door open so I can get some air?" But they would not. So I took off my clothes, sat down and waited while I read the scriptures. I didn't hear the elevator go up and down and decided they hadn't gone anywhere. They were still in the building, just across the hall.

In the room across the corridor from our prison, the room in which the guards lived, David Jacobson was making a videotape using the same script we all used in the segment of our previous tape directed to the U.S. government.

I was still reading when Hajj came in and through his interpreter told me, "I want you to tell the Holy Father what the Christians do here in the Middle East. They are broadcasting immoral ads and programs on their television. They show frontal nudity of women, and that is offensive to us as people of Islam. It is especially bad for our children. Ask the Holy Father to intervene to stop these commercials and programs that the Christians broadcast."

Hajj also told me to speak to President Reagan and to ask for the freedom of the seventeen imprisoned in Kuwait for their attacks on the American and French embassies. Some were sentenced to death.

Hajj also questioned why Christians and Muslims couldn't get along better. "We believe in the same God. We have the same father in faith, Abraham. We reverence Jesus as a great prophet and Mary, his virgin mother. And we basically have the same moral code."

"Why," he asked, "can't we build on what is common to us, instead of tearing each other apart because of our differences?"

Sayeed advised me to take my Dyazide pills. Alarmed at what this could mean I said, "Sayeed, they're not going to tape me up like a mummy again and put me under a truck to move me, are they?" He didn't respond at all.

I wanted the three letters I had received as a hostage—the letter from Sister Bernadine, a letter from Tom Namaya who had worked for CRS, and the other from my nephew, David. These letters were very important to me, sustaining me in times of loneliness and despair. I had reread them a thousand times.

I also wanted to carry out the journal I kept. At first I planned to stash all these in my shorts and walk out with them. But then I thought, "Oh, I better not do that." So I asked Hajj if I could carry them out, and he said no. He instructed me to carry only the videotape that David was making and to give it to the Associated Press, "and no one else. If the Syrian government takes it away from you, we will kill the American hostages."

My response was, "Hajj, first of all, I never expected the Syrians were going to be involved in all this; but your very mention of them indicates you suspect they will take it away from me no matter what I tell them. What happens if they do? It's not fair to kill the Americans because the Syrians take away a videotape."

Hajj said, "Well, if the Syrians take it away from you, you must let me know it at your first press conference. But it must be shown this day by the Associated Press, or we will kill the other Americans."

I was very anxious about being so responsible for the other hostages in such uncertain conditions. It terrified me to think their lives should hang on my successfully dodging the Syrian army and safely delivering a videotape to the A.P. How could I reasonably be expected to accomplish such a thing? For the past nineteen months I hadn't even so much as visited the toilet under my own volition!

Then I stood in my shorts in front of Hajj, and he read a letter to me.

> Dear brothers and sisters,
>
> If I am to die I hope that I will die with the words of Jesus on my lips, "Father, forgive them; for they do no know what they are doing." Please do not hate them and if you want to know where I am spiritually, read Psalms 116, 117, and 118.

I recognized my Christmas letter and realized it had never been sent. Hajj did not read it to me because he wanted me to know it had not been sent; rather he used its words to ask for forgiveness.

He made one more request, "Please give our condolences to Ben Weir's family on the death of his beautiful daughter and to Terry Anderson's family on the death of his father and brother," and left the room. Perhaps that had been the reason they would not give us back the radio. They didn't want us to hear that Terry's father and brother, and Ben's daughter Ann had died. They didn't think that we could cope with it.

One of the effects of being sealed alone in an overheated room is that you can easily lose any accurate sense of time's passage. It seemed as if I had been waiting for hours. I wasn't even sure I was really going home. I feared it might end like so many previous times when they dressed me up, left me waiting, then told me they were just kidding. I kept saying "Oh God, please let this be true. Let this be true."

Then suddenly they entered the room bringing me my last hostage meal—spaghetti. It was cold, but I was hungry and ate it thinking I would need the sustenance for what lay ahead. I kept reading the scriptures. I opened to Chapter 36 of Ezekiel.

> A new heart I will give you, and a new spirit I will put within you; and I will remove from your body the heart of stone and give you a heart of flesh. I will put my spirit within you, and make you follow my statutes and be careful to observe my ordinances. Then you shall live in the land that I gave to your ancestors; and you shall be my people, and I will be your God (26-28).

It really became a prayer for me:

> God, give me a new heart and a new spirit. You have asked me to love unconditionally. May I forgive as you have asked me to forgive, unconditionally. Then you will be my God and I will be your son.

CHAPTER ELEVEN

A CROSS TO LIVE

Lord, by your cross and resurrection you have set me free,
you are the savior of the world.
                                                    —From the Mass

Five hundred and sixty-four days after my kidnapping, in the last of my many prisons, I am standing, blindfolded, in front of an elevator, dressed to go home. Two guards, Abu Ali and Mahmoud, stand behind me. In an adjacent room are my brother hostages who are not going home. When David was making the tape, Hajj told him I was being released and would be carrying out the tape. So they know. No farewells were permitted.

Abu Ali says, "Here, Abouna," and I feel him place something in my hand which I recognize immediately to be a small cross. How strange. On the morning of my kidnapping I wore a treasured silver chain and cross that a brother Servite had given me on my twenty-fifth anniversary as a priest. One of my kidnappers had taken it from me. From the first to the last of my captivity, I had no cross. It was as if God had said, "I'm going to give you a cross to live instead of the one you wear."

Abu Ali's gift closes a circle—and it's so shocking to me. I think of Tom Dooley. When he died in 1961 working in Laos, he carried a prayer from his sister in his wallet. It was called "Your Cross."

> The everlasting God has in his wisdom foreseen
> from eternity the cross that he now presents to you
> as a gift from his innermost heart. The cross he now
> sends you he has considered with his all-knowing
> eyes, understood with his divine mind, tested with

his wise justice, warmed with loving arms, weighed with his own hands, to see that it be not one inch too large and not one ounce too heavy for you. He has blessed it with his holy name, anointed it with his grace, perfumed it with his consolation, taken one last glance at you and your courage and then sent it to you from heaven, a special greeting from God to you, and alms of the all-merciful God.

I thought about this prayer in captivity. At this moment Abu Ali's gift has me wondering, "Why, God, now this cross?" As if to reassure me in my silent questioning, Mahmoud—a guard who had been with me from the beginning—stands behind me massaging my shoulders. And I remember this young man standing next to me the morning of my kidnapping. I had looked into his eyes and saw the eyes of hate, a look that never left me. It was etched into my mind. He had said, "You are dead!" And I had asked, "Why do you say that?" He did not respond.

Now he massages me with a gentle, gentle touch—not one of violence but of compassion. I want very much to lift my blindfold just to look into his eyes. I know that I would not see the eyes of hatred as I did that first morning. This was his way of apologizing and I believe I would have looked into the eyes of love.

I'm in the elevator going down. Abu Ali is with me. At the bottom floor he exits with me, escorts me to the waiting van, and gets in with me. They drive me to a garage as Abu Ali tells me, "Abouna, now I can go home." He tells me the Israelis killed his parents and he made a commitment to guard me. Since I was going home, so could he. But I'll find out from the other hostages after their release that Abu Ali was around for some time after my release. In a way, our being held captive turned our guards into hostages, too.

They back the van into a garage, take me out, and sit me on a piece of cardboard. I'm on the ground for an hour or so before I hear, "Please stand up." I hold my new cross in the palm of my hand. Someone instructs me: "Put your ankles close together and your arms to your side." Once again they tape up my body. I'm saying, "Oh, God, please don't." But they wrap me from my ankles to the top of my head.

When they reach my mouth, someone says, "Open your mouth." They had always placed a cloth gag in my mouth in previous transportations so I couldn't make any noise. But this time it's not a gag. It's the two Dyazide pills Sayeed wanted me to take so I would survive my last trip pretending to be a spare tire. I swallow the pills and they tape my face except for my nostrils so I can breathe.

They slide me under the bed of the truck into the spare tire compartment. It's hard to breathe and I have to fight panic. Now I know one reason for the gift cross as I manipulate it so as to cut the tape and free a hand. Now I peel the rest of the tape off. My body is free. I brace myself against the steel walls of the compartment so I won't be slammed around so hard. "God, make this trip be short!" I pray, but it's not. By the time they stop, my hands are bloody.

As they transfer me to a car, they tell me to keep the blindfold on, push me down onto the floor of the car, but make no comment about the tape being gone. They drive for some time, then stop at an out-of-the-way spot. They dump me at the roadside and tell me not to remove my blindfold for fifteen minutes after they leave. They give me the videotape and tell me not to give it to the "Syrian dogs. Tell the Syrian dogs that we hate them."

In captivity, the guards would sometimes ask me, "Is there anything you want?" and I would say, "A taxicab home." On this 26th day of July, the Feast of Saints Joachim and Anne, I hear the words, "Here, Abouna, over your head. Five Lebanese pounds. Catch your taxicab and go home." I ask, "Which way is home?" "To the left."

Then I hear the sounds of car doors closing, the ignition, and tires crunching away in the dust. I "guesstimate" when fifteen minutes are up and I lift my blindfold.

In the distance, I saw mountains, a lake, a village. I prayed the prayer of the three young men in the fiery furnace who sang in one voice, glorifying and blessing God (cf. Daniel 3:50-90):

"Sky, bless the Lord. Earth, bless the Lord. Water, bless the Lord. Seas, bless the Lord. Dolphins, bless the Lord." I felt in no hurry as I sat looking at God's creation for the first time in almost nineteen months.

After a while I started to walk along the road in the direction the guard told me—toward a small village on a hill. I was dehydrated and getting anxious, but I kept telling myself not to worry, as if my presence would attract no attention whatever. After all, why, in this remote spot somewhere along the Lebanese-Syrian border, would the appearance of a Caucasian in western dress, with strips of tape hanging off his back, clumps of cotton padding in his hair, pants zipper broken, plastic bag in hand, not be an everyday thing?

I came by a family working in front of their home adjacent to the road. The women wore traditional headgear and I thought they looked like Shiites so I was a bit frightened. I asked in Arabic, "Is there a church nearby?" and they said, "Yes, up on the mountain."

On the way I met two young men and asked them the same question. They pointed the same direction. Halfway there, a man pulled up in a car and offered a ride. I asked him to take me to the church. As he dropped me off he said, "Why do you want to go to this church? There are no Christians left in this village."

I crossed the street to a little shop and bought a cola. I asked the shopkeeper, "Where is the nearest place to catch a taxicab or bus to Beirut?" I wanted to go back to Beirut and depart Lebanon through the Vatican embassy. I had no idea where I was. And people in the store wouldn't tell me.

Someone brought a Christian man to me. He pulled up in a big, old car and walked over to see me. I told him I was a Roman Catholic American priest who had just been released. Then strangely, and with tremendous sadness rooted in his fear, he said to me, "Abouna, I am so sorry, but I cannot help you." He got back into his car and drove away.

Then a young man came up to me and in English said to follow him. He wouldn't walk beside me. I had to follow behind him. He brought me to a police station. I told the policeman at the desk who I was and I sat down. That's when I discovered my zipper was broken. I leaned across the desk, picked up a stapler, and stapled the front of my pants shut. They wanted to know what I had in my plastic bag. "It's a videotape I must give to no one except the Associated Press." They didn't insist on taking it from me.

Then I had to go to the toilet. They thought it was funny as I carried the plastic bag with me. What I saw in the mirror of that restroom was quite bizarre. How frightening I must have looked to the people I'd encountered thus far! After I emerged from the toilet, and while I waited for the police to figure out what they were going to do with me, I picked the cotton threads off my head and removed the strips of tape that were still hanging from my clothes. I also restapled my zipper.

I just couldn't get anywhere with those men. They didn't seem to understand my story and I started to cry. That got them very agitated. They brought in a very attractive woman, wearing traditional headgear, who spoke English very well. She said to me, "Abouna, you don't have to worry. You are safe here." I suppose this was her way of letting me know that the Syrians were on their way.

Within a few minutes, soldiers arrived and loaded me into a jeep. We stopped at a Syrian checkpoint somewhere on the way to Damascus. Without asking me what was in the plastic bag, they simply ripped it from my hands. I told them, "I'm to give that to the Associated Press." They responded, "We'll give it back to you." Needless to say, I had my doubts.

We stopped at an army installation of some sort. My new captors ushered me into a room where I had the privilege to be scrutinized by a general who sat looking back and forth between me and a picture of me that had been published in the Arabic news.

"It doesn't look like the same person," he commented. How strange I thought. After nineteen months of subsistent existence in captivity and forgoing the joys of shaving, I didn't look like the clean-shaven man in the picture. Suddenly I was unleashed, fully bearded, on the defenseless Syrian army, and he was quite puzzled.

Somehow he figured out I should be taken to Damascus. So they loaded me back in the jeep, without the videotape, for a twenty-minute ride.

In Damascus, they brought me to a government building. As I sat and waited, I didn't feel free. Without the videotape and bound by my former captors' threat, I was quite anxious. The situation totally vitiated any sense of exhilaration I might have experienced at my release. I kept asking for my tape. Then wearily I said to a young man sitting at a desk, "I just feel so dirty. May I clean up?"

He rose from his chair, opened a closet, pulled out a white, tropical suit, and gave it to me saying, "I think this will fit you." I'm sure the suit was his. He also gave me a toothbrush and toothpaste.

I showered, brushed my teeth, and donned the suit, dropping my old clothes on the floor. They were very dirty from my trip beneath the truck. I only kept the socks and shoes. I looked at the clothes and said to myself, "It's over now. Leave them there." Purifications and ablutions completed, I stepped over the shed skin of my hostage existence into my new yet old life.

I reentered the waiting room to a table set with all kinds of food—food I hadn't seen in over nineteen months—but in my anxiety I couldn't eat. I picked up one item and they said, "That's dessert. You shouldn't eat that just yet. You should eat something more stable." But it looked good so I ate it.

Finally I said, "I want to go home." They said, "You're going home soon. We're waiting for the American ambassador to turn you over to him." They brought in some of their own intelligence agents to interview me. Then the Syrians wanted to know the names of my captors and how I got there. I told them, "They wrapped me up with tape like a mummy, put me in the tire rack under a truck, and dropped me off somewhere nearby—and here I am."

Next they took me to be turned over to the American ambassador. When I arrived, I was surprised to find hordes of journalists and photographers waiting, and wondered how they even knew my whereabouts. The first person to greet me and give me a hug was Peg Say, Terry Anderson's sister, who had been in Damascus trying to mediate our release. We were escorted to a room in the building where I was to be turned over to the American officials where we had a few minutes together.

I told her Terry was okay and aware of her efforts. I also told her about the videotape and the threat to kill the hostages if it was not broadcast by midnight. I also extended the condolences from Hajj. Then she sort of disappeared as I went to the meeting of Syrian and American officials for the exchange and a press conference.

Actually, Peg went back to her hotel and called the Associated Press to tell them about the tape. In tracing it, A.P. found out that American officials had gotten it from the Syrians and were making copies so they could study it. She reminded them of Hajj's threat. After a confrontation with American officials, the Associated Press got the tape and rushed it to the one television station in Damascus where it was broadcast on time.

The first thing I told the ambassador, after meeting him, was that the Syrians had taken the videotape I was to give to the Associated Press. If I didn't get it to A.P., I explained, "They're going to kill the other American hostages. I want the tape. It has to be shown today. Would you promise me that?" And he said, "Yes, we'll get the tape for you. Don't worry about it."

I didn't know exactly what time of day it was. It seemed still to be morning, but I wasn't sure. After being turned over, I was then escorted to the American embassy residence.

When I arrived at the American embassy, Alan Kempchar, who was with the State Department, was standing just inside in the door. "Hi, Marty," he greeted me. It was a pleasant surprise from a gentle God to almost immediately see the face of a friend. I knew Alan while living in North Yemen, working with Mother Teresa's sisters and Catholic Relief Services. He attended Mass regularly either at the American embassy or at the German farm there. I also baptized one of his babies, I believe.

The officials then brought me in to meet the ambassador's wife and children. Alan took some photos—he was a consul and was preparing a passport for me. When I look at that passport photo, I see the day of my release, and the lovely smile of a man once bound, now free.

I then took some sacred time for myself, after which the Apostolic Nuncio to Syria showed up and asked if I would like to receive the eucharist. I said, "Yes." He left, returning to the Vatican embassy in Syria, and reappeared shortly. We knelt and prayed, and I received Jesus. It was a rather emotional encounter with the Lord. He also asked if I wanted to return home wearing a clerical suit and I said yes.

The suit he provided was about four sizes larger than I normally wear. The jacket more or less billowed around my upper body and I had to hold the pants up with suspenders. I felt sort of Charlie Chaplin-esque. But I didn't care. It was just so overwhelming and refreshing to know that I was going home.

Next I called my family in Joliet. I had dreamt of returning home, walking in through the back door of my sister's place and simply saying, "Hi, I'm home." Talking to my brothers and sisters, nieces and nephews, was quite special, something I dreamt of in captivity. But when the reality was there, I didn't know what to say except, "Hi. I'm okay." I found out they were coming to Wiesbaden to meet me.

I was asked if there was any special food I would like for dinner. How I had obsessed about food in captivity, dreamt about all the wonderful things God has given us for nourishment. Now I had a choice of anything I wanted. I love hot, spicy food so I asked for Mexican, and I asked to eat outside. I didn't want to eat within the confines of a room on this first day of freedom.

A Mexican meal was prepared that evening and served outdoors. As I approached the serving table and looked over the wonderful banquet I was completely astonished. At the end of that table full of Mexican food sat a bowl of pickled herring! How could this be? I had told no one of my recurrent dream. I suppose a gentle God was letting me know that I was free.

CHAPTER TWELVE

FREE AND YET NOT FREE

I am your servant, the child of your servant girl.
You have loosed my bonds.
To you will I offer to you a thanksgiving sacrifice
and I will call upon the name of the Lord.
                                    —Psalm 116:16-17

My first night of freedom was a night of rediscoveries, among them the beauty and joy of women and children. Not having seen a feminine face for over nineteen months, I found myself staring at women. I remember apologizing to one woman, "I'm sorry I stare. I haven't seen the face of a woman for nineteen months and your face is so beautiful." The ambassador's children were there also, which added another joyful dimension to the night.

The next morning the Apostolic Nuncio and I celebrated eucharist with those who wished to be present. There was something particularly moving about celebrating with him.

In the midst of all the activity surrounding my "reappearance," I wrote two letters—one to Pope John Paul, the other to President Reagan—on the subjects Hajj and I had discussed prior to my release. It never occurred to me that I would get the chance to see the Pope or the President, so I gave the letters to American and Vatican diplomats in Syria to pass on to the President and the Pope.

Somehow the word "secret" became attached to this correspondence. But my decision to send these messages in this fashion had nothing to do with secrecy. I simply preferred private

122

correspondence so it was a complete surprise to me that any intrigue developed around it. Apparently many people felt they had a right to know the contents of a personal communication from Hajj through me to the President and the Pope. Others felt an open letter would create more interest concerning the plight of the remaining hostages.

I shared the goal of keeping the plight of the hostages in the public eye. My accepting invitations to Rome and Washington had precisely to do with this concern. Several months prior to my release, I had promised Terry Anderson that, if I were released first, he would not be forgotten. This was a solemn covenant between us.

My departure from Damascus was a bit frantic contrary to my expectations. I had envisioned my captors dropping me off somewhere in Beirut. I'd then find my way to a hotel, call my family, and catch a plane home. I didn't expect this tremendous apparatus in place to bring me back to the United States via Wiesbaden, Germany. It included a special military medevac plane full of doctors and nurses, and a psychiatrist who did little more than sit next to me during the flight.

I didn't want my family to meet me at Wiesbaden. I wanted to meet them at home, in a familiar environment. I didn't want to meet them at a government hospital and was saddened it couldn't have been otherwise.

We touched down in Wiesbaden amid tremendous press coverage, which still amazes me. I was greeted by many important people while hospital staff members and patients stood on balconies waving flags and cheering. It was all so overwhelming.

I was brought to a very nice two-room suite in the hospital where a guard was posted outside my door. A big bowl of fruit sat on a coffee table in the sitting room. How I had dreamed repeatedly as a hostage of eating fresh fruit. On this occasion I didn't eat any of it. I just gazed at it intently even while everyone was there and after they had left.

The hospital staff checked my health and for the most part I was in good shape. The unhappy condition of my teeth occasioned the worst of my physical complaints.

I was also interviewed and debriefed by American State Department and CIA officials. They exerted no great pressure. They just asked basic questions like what had I eaten in captivity? Who were my captors? Where had I been kept? And did I experience any violence?

One day I was standing in the bedroom of my suite without knowing my family had arrived and were in the adjacent room. I opened the door and there they all were. We shared tears, embraces and hugs, laughter and stories.

I remained very fearful of certain things. Despite the assurances of the American ambassador in Syria, I was very conscious of not knowing what had happened to the video or if it had been broadcast. Also, before my release, my captors had threatened to kill me, "If ever we see you drinking alcohol," which made me very anxious around alcohol. One evening, officials videotaped a family dinner celebration in the base cafeteria. My anxiety was heightened by the sound of corks popping in the background. So instead of feeling completely liberated, I still had these fears—personal fear and fear for my brother hostages.

My family took me clothes shopping. I couldn't find a black suit so I bought a dark blue pinstripe. Terry Waite gave me a watch because my kidnappers never returned mine. Although appreciative, I had learned a different attitude about things while in captivity. "Cling to nothing" became my motto.

The medical tests and debriefings continued until it was time to leave. I was anxious to go home, but Terry Waite, whom I had met in Damascus during my first meal in freedom, wanted me to go to England to meet the Archbishop of Canterbury, then to Rome to meet Vatican officials and the Pope. I knew that my family had never been to Europe and I was pleased that this would allow them to visit both London and Rome.

The morning of our departure we gave praise and thanks to a gentle God for my release and asked God for the release of the other hostages. In the chapel where we gathered, the Bible was lying open on the altar. I walked up to the altar to select a text and was stunned to find that it was open precisely at Psalms 116, 117, and 118, the very psalms I had mentioned in my unmailed Christmas love letter to my family. Turning to my brothers and sisters and the other staff members I asked, "Did anyone touch this Bible?" and they said, "No. Didn't you notice? The windows are open and the wind blew in and turned the pages." These psalms became our prayers of praise and thanksgiving that morning.

After flying into London, we first went to Westminster to meet Archbishop Robert Runcie. My family received a tour of his residence while the Archbishop and I sat in a comfortable room and shared stories. I sensed an air of anticipation, as if someone was due to arrive. I was right and to my great surprise and joy, Ben Weir was ushered into the room. He had been in Europe at the time of my release and flew in from Germany to see me. He had only a short time before a departing flight, but they were precious moments for us both.

We all went to the chapel to pray, to give thanks and praise for Ben's and my release, and to pray for the release of the other hostages. My visit and talk with Archbishop Runcie stays with me. He was a huggy man, both very approachable and very prayerful. Of all the photos taken during this time, I greatly cherish the one of the two of us standing side by side.

That evening we celebrated eucharist in the church of St. Mary's. Afterward, at a reception for me, I met Jill Morrell, the fiancee of the British hostage John McCarthy. I basically encouraged her to trust in the Lord that John would survive and be released. I was beginning to understand that my presence to the loved ones of those still in captivity gave them courage. They sensed that if I survived, so would John, David, Tom, and Terry.

The next day my family toured London while I stayed at the Servite Priory with my community brothers, free to sleep and rest, to use the toilet when I chose, to get a glass of water when thirsty, to eat when hungry, and not have to squirrel away food.

From London we flew to Rome and stayed at St. Alexis

Servite College, known as the Marianum, where I had attended college from 1955 to 1959. I think I even stayed in my old room.

The next day I was taken to the residence of the American Ambassador to the Vatican who introduced me to two secretaries to Pope John Paul II. For several hours they questioned me about my ordeal and I communicated to them Hajj's message to the Holy Father. Their questioning exhausted me, complicated by the fact that I was trying to deal with my anger over the church's inactivity regarding the hostages.

I had learned that the families of the hostages had organized prayer vigils, created posters, buttons, yellow lapel ribbons, and anniversary awareness days. They appeared on television and radio talk shows and secured assistance from congressmen and senators, Protestant and Catholic clerics. They were involved with two organizations, "No Greater Love" and "Points of Lights," which had done tremendous work keeping the plight of the hostages in the public eye. But through all these efforts they were saddened by the inactivity and resistance of the government and the church.

This sadness was relieved in great measure by a private audience with the Pope which meant a great deal to them. One of the secretaries gave me a letter to give to the Pope in our audience. I was to tell him that the contents of my conversation with the two secretaries was in this letter, so I wouldn't have to go into any detail about what was said.

When the Holy Father entered the hall, he was clearly very tired. He had just returned from one of his journeys. I met with him first, and then introduced my family and friends. My brothers and sisters had a chance to shake his hand and kiss his ring and speak to him. It was a holy day that helped the healing process for my family.

A day or so later, we flew to Washington, D.C. where I was welcomed home by CRS staff and the senators from my home state of Illinois. It was very nice to recognize some familiar faces from my pilgrimage of dreams and to see and touch them in the flesh. At a reception I met William Buckley's sisters. I told them what I believed had happened to him and how he died. Sadly, this family would not have a homecoming for their loved one.

I met with President Reagan in the Oval Office along with Mrs. Reagan, Secretary of State George Schultz, and Ambassador Oakley. At least those are the people I recall. Later, during the Iran-Contra scandal, I was asked if I ever met Oliver North, and I said I had not. My nephew Andrew Mihelich called me on the phone later and said, "Uncle Larry, I have an 8" x 10" photograph of you taken when you met with the President. One of the men in that room was Ollie North." I guess his presence was not particularly memorable to me.

There was little conversation during my Oval Office visit. The President was distant, Oakley and North said nothing, and Schultz made a comment something to the effect that "I guess prayer works."

Mrs. Reagan on the other hand displayed the kind of compassion that women have and men often seem incapable of expressing. She talked with me in a way that helped pull out some of the pain, asking me understanding questions about my imprisonment. It was exactly what I needed in the process of healing my memories at that time.

Other than that, basically I shared this letter with them:

Dear President Reagan:

An hour before I left my last prison, the leader of the group that held us hostage these past months verbally gave me messages to give to His Holiness Pope John Paul II, to you, and the families of Terry Anderson, David Jacobson, and Thomas Sutherland. He also wished me to convey to the Anderson family their condolences on the deaths of Terry Anderson's father and brother and their condolences to Rev. Ben Weir on the tragic death of his daughter in Cairo, Egypt.

The message that I was to give to you was to be confidential and I was to divulge its contents to no one else but you and the families of the remaining three Americans and ask them to hold this message in strictest confidence. I wish, Mr. President, that I could be a bearer of good news. The message, Mr. President, is: "The condition for the release of Mr. Terry Anderson, Mr. David Jacobson, and Mr. Thomas Sutherland is the release of the seventeen being held in Kuwait. Their lives and the lives of other Americans are dependent on that condition being realized . . . and soon."

They believe that all you have to do, Mr. President, is pick up the phone and call the Emir of Kuwait and tell him to set the seventeen free. I wish it were that easy.

One hour prior to that final conversation another leader informed me of the deaths of Terry Anderson's father and brother and of Rev. Ben Weir's daughter. He also said that they killed Mr. William Buckley because he was an evil man, he was the head of the C.I.A. in that region of the world. I personally believe Mr. Buckley died a natural death and my captors want other radical groups to believe they did execute him.

Both leaders asked forgiveness from me for the nineteen months of suffering I had to endure; both quoted the final words of Jesus: "Father, forgive them for they know not what they do." Also they expressed their sadness about the kidnappings. They know kidnapping is wrong but they have no other forum to present their cause to the world.

They also asked that the American government's foreign policy in the Middle East be just. Presently, it is one-sided: pro-Israel. And not all Arabs are oil millionaires. There are millions of poor Arabs in the Middle East who have legitimate human needs and rights that are denied them.

My captors in those final minutes stressed that

they do not want the Syrians to be involved in any negotiations on the release of the other three Americans.

I have given you the message that I gave the Pope in Rome, John Paul II. I do this so that you know its contents. I did not tell them of the condition of the seventeen of Kuwait. I am sure they know.

I pray to our dearest God I have recalled well those final conversations and I have honestly conveyed their messages.

Mr. President, there were times I did not have kind and charitable thoughts about my government, my Servite order, my church, and the CRS. I have asked God's forgiveness for these sinful [thoughts] and ask your forgiveness, too. Thank you for your prayers and all that you have done on our behalf.

In the future, I might still get angry—bear with me.

May the God of Abraham, Isaac, and Jacob, of Jesus, of Mohammed, our God, answer our prayers for the release of our fellow Americans . . . still held hostage somewhere.

> With gratitude.
> Father Lawrence Martin Jenco
> Servite

While in Washington, we stayed at the Carmelite monastery at Whitefriars Hall where my nephew was a seminarian. We were very grateful for the Carmelite hospitality which included a wonderful reception for friends and acquaintances in the D.C. area and CRS friends with whom I had worked in various parts of the world.

We then returned to Joliet by ordinary commercial flight where we were welcomed with a big parade. I don't think there was a store window or an arcade without a poster reading, "Welcome home, Father Jenco!" Thousands of people attended a gathering at an old restored theater. Among those on stage was the Rev. Jesse Jackson, one of the first persons to offer assistance to my family after I was kidnapped. He had always been very kind to them and they were very grateful for all his efforts on behalf of the hostages.

During my first week home in Joliet I met with the families of David Jacobson, Tom Sutherland, and Terry Anderson. It was so good to meet them, to see and touch the faces of those who had only been subjects of conversations behind a locked door in a sealed room.

By CRS arrangement I saw a psychiatrist for several months on a weekly basis, just to unwind. This was good for me in that it helped me understand the pain and suffering in the hearts and souls of a hostage's loved ones. My brothers and sisters, too, needed someone to help them close the wounds of this nineteen-month trauma. I'm not too sure they have been able to yet. They were deeply pained by the events. They were on a nonstop emotional roller coaster propelled by rumors—now of my release, now of my death, now of the threats of execution. My brothers and sisters travelled around the country to speak on my behalf and on the behalf of the other hostages and bonded deeply with the families of other hostages.

From my first day home I looked for news of the other hostages and any news would get my attention. At times I would be sitting in my sister's living room with my little grand-nieces and -nephews around, and something about me would appear on television. Too young to grasp what was occurring, they would see my image on the screen and then they'd turn and look at me. In some ways, their utterly quizzical and uncomprehending faces summed up a bizarre phase of my life.

Epilog

I belong to a religious community called the Servants of Mary, or Servites, founded over 750 years ago by seven Florentine noblemen to be a sign in a world torn by religious and political strife. That remains our mission.

Less than five months prior to my kidnapping I celebrated my twenty-fifth anniversary as a priest among family and friends in my boyhood parish of St. Bernard's in Joliet. In my anniversary homily that day, I explained that:

> God's gift of priesthood and the irrevocable call to servanthood have taken me to many peoples: American, Indian, Australian Aborigine, Mexican, Yemeni, Thai, Khmer, Vietnamese, Hmong, Laotians. To many places, to many cultures, to many religions—Hindu, Buddhist, Muslim, Christian.
>
> The Lord Jesus gifted us with the sacraments of eucharist and priesthood on the evening of his death. I believe that one should not separate these sacraments from his command to be, as he was, a servant, a towel and basin person, a man for others.

The concept of servanthood is very much a part of my understanding of priesthood. As I was preparing to go to Beirut, a city torn by religious and political factions, I asked those present to pray with me that the charisms of the founders of my community, men of peace and reconciliation, would be passed on to me; that I might be a reconciler, a person of peace, and help bring the warring sides together. I asked them to pray with me that my life would be an incarnation of truth, for the Lord Jesus said, "If you say you love God whom you do not see and hate your neighbor whom you do see, you are a liar."

I closed that homily with praise and thanks "for the nourishment of relatives and friends, who, in the past, today, and

131

tomorrow, have nourished, nourish, and will nourish us in our faith in God's covenant promise: Jesus."

In the days of captivity, chained to a wall, I found myself asking God in a silent shout, "Why? Why me!" My nourishment in this loneliness was God's word and God's table, and the awareness that my family and friends, and my brother Servites all remembered me. Holding onto the eucharistic Christ, I would recall the words of Jesus: "Do this in remembrance of me." Holding onto Christ I would say "Jesus, don't forget me." And I would be aware of those eyes of compassion looking on me, both the eyes of Jesus and the eyes of my mother.

Early in this book I mentioned that the guards gave me a copy of Camus' *The Plague*. Two scenes from it still surface in my dreams. The book is a story of Oran, a town held hostage by a ravaging epidemic of bubonic plague. Quarantined from the outside world, this Algerian port city becomes a prison of disease and death.

The first scene involves a Sunday High Mass. A Jesuit priest, Father Paneloux, is asked to preach the homily. His opening statement seems to be the core of his sermon: "Calamity has come on you, my brethren, and my brethren, you deserved it." He further develops this initial statement—with a voice low and vibrant with accusation:

> Yes, the hour has come for serious thought. You fondly imagined it was enough to visit God on Sundays, and thus you could make free of your weekdays. You believed some brief formalities, some bendings of the knee, would recompense him well enough for your criminal indifference. But God is not mocked. These brief encounters could not sate the fierce hunger of his love. . . . And this is why, wearied of waiting for you to come to him, he loosed on you this visitation; as he has visited all the cities that offended against him since the dawn of history. Now you are learning your lesson, the lesson that

was learned by Cain and his offspring, by the people
of Sodom and Gomorrah, by Job and Pharaoh, by
all that hardened their hearts against him. . . .

Now, at last, you know the hour has struck to
bend your thoughts to first and last things.

Quarantined from the fabric of my own life and identity, as
well as the world outside; facing the possibility of death at the
hands of my captors, I stopped reading and reflected about God,
my life, my holiness, my sinfulness. Are past, present, and future
plagues the wrath of a vengeful God? Mentally I expanded the
concept of plague to include all those chains that bind us: poverty, mental and physical illnesses, ignorance, addictions, physical
disabilities, governments, and religions. I found myself wondering. Perhaps my own captivity was God's way of teaching me a
lesson about what it means to be bound. Perhaps I did not do
enough for the Indochinese refugees. I went into the border
camps, but I was free to leave. The refugees, some for many
years, still remained imprisoned.

But then I would think, "This is not the God of the New
Testament. My God is Love. Love wouldn't do this." And so I
offered that prayer of love and trusted a gentle God to see to the
rest.

In the other scene Father Paneloux witnesses a child dying
from the plague, "and from the day on which he saw a child die,
something seemed to change him." He gave another sermon, but
instead of saying, "you," he said, "we." He didn't reject his first
sermon, but realized that "what a Christian should always seek
in his hour of trial is to discern the good."

In his second sermon Paneloux tried to explain the phe-
nomenon of plague and learn what it has to teach us:

> There was no doubt as to the existence of good and
> evil and, as a rule, it was easy to see the difference
> between them. The difficulty began when we looked
> into the nature of evil, and among things evil he
> (God) included human suffering. Thus we had
> apparently needful pain, and apparently needless

pain; we had Don Juan cast into hell, and a child's death. . . .

My brothers . . . the love of God is a hard love. It demands total self-surrender; disdain of our human personality. And yet it alone can reconcile us to suffering and the deaths of children, it alone can justify them, since we cannot understand them, and we can only make God's will ours. That is the hard lesson I would share with you today. That is the faith, cruel in men's eyes, and crucial in God's, which we must ever strive to compass. We must aspire beyond ourselves toward that high and fearful vision. And on that lofty plane all will fall into place, all discords be resolved, and truth flash forth from the dark cloud of seeming injustice.

In my own plague I claim the words of the narrator of Camus's book, Dr. Rieux. With Rieux I offer my account, "So that some memorial of the injustice and outrage done them might endure; and to state quite simply what we learn in time of pestilence: that there are more things to admire in men than despise."

In this experience of forgiveness I have struggled with my anger. I forgave my captors, and they forgave me. But I remember my anger—with my guards, with Hajj, and with the other hostages. In response to my outbursts my captors would retaliate in hurtful ways—no food, no radio, no newspaper. In the quiet of my heart I'd speak to God: "Perhaps I wasn't slow with my anger? Perhaps I sinned?" The psalmist writes that our God is merciful and gracious, slow to anger, abounding in kindness. Isn't there both good, healthy, constructive anger, and bad, unhealthy, destructive anger?

In his book *Making Friends of Enemies* Jim Forest offers insight into my struggle when he points out that forgiveness may be a wonderful thing, "But what about anger? Haven't I a right to my anger? When I am hurt, should I pretend not to feel the hurt? And if I manage to pretend, to hide my hurt and anger, am I not lying?" He goes on to say that forgiveness that masks the pain and rage is of no value.

> Until we allow ourselves to feel the hurt and to express it, it is unlikely an act of forgiveness will be genuine. If the forgiveness we seek to offer to those who need our forgiveness is to be of any use to them, they need to be aware of what they have done and the pain or hurt it has caused.

Some people advise me to forgive and forget. They do not realize that this is almost impossible. Jesus, the wounded healer, asks us to forgive, but he does not ask us to forget. That would be amnesia. He does demand we heal our memories.

I don't believe that forgetting is one of the signs of forgiveness. I forgive, but I remember. I do not forget the pain, the loneliness, the ache, the terrible injustice. But I do not remember it to inflict guilt or some future retribution. Having forgiven, I am liberated. I need no longer be determined by the past. I move into the future free to imagine new possibilities.